ABOUT THE AUTHOR

Jill Spencer was for several years chief home economist in the
Hamlyn Publishing Group's test kitchen, where she supervised
recipe testing and food photography. She studied home
economics at the Croydon College of Design and Technology
and afterwards worked for a well-known food manufacturer.
She performed extensive experiments with microwave cookery
in the test kitchen while developing the recipes in this book.

CW00549877

MICROWAVE COOKBOOK

The complete guide to a
new way of cooking

Jill Spencer

Arrow Books Limited
17–21 Conway Street, London W1P 6JD

An imprint of the Hutchinson Publishing Group

London Melbourne Sydney Auckland
Johannesburg and agencies throughout the world

First published in Great Britain by
The Hamlyn Publishing Group Ltd 1978
Hamlyn Paperbacks edition 1982
Reprinted 1982
Arrow edition 1985
© The Hamlyn Publishing Group Ltd 1978

Printed and bound in Great Britain by
Cox & Wyman Ltd, Reading

ISBN 0 09 940580 6

Contents

Useful facts and figures

Notes on metrication
Exact conversion from Imperial to metric measures does not usually give very convenient working quantities and so the metric measures have been rounded off into units of 25 grams. The table below shows the recommended equivalents.

Ounces	Approx g to nearest whole figure	Recommended conversion to nearest unit of 25
1	28	25
2	57	50
3	85	75
4	113	100
5	142	150
6	170	175
7	198	200
8	227	225
9	255	250
10	283	275
11	312	300
12	340	350
13	368	375
14	396	400
15	425	425
16 (1 lb)	454	450
17	482	475
18	510	500
19	539	550
20 (1¼ lb)	567	575

Note When converting quantities over 20 oz first add the appropriate figures in the centre column, then adjust to the nearest unit of 25. As a general guide, 1 kg (1000 g) equals 2·2 lb or about 2 lb 3 oz. This method of conversion gives good results in nearly all cases, although in certain pastry and cake recipes a more accurate conversion is necessary to produce a balanced recipe.

Liquid measures The millilitre has been used in this book and the following table gives a few examples.

Imperial	Approx ml to nearest whole figure	Recommended ml
¼ pint	142	150ml
½ pint	283	300 ml
¾ pint	425	450 ml
1 pint	567	600 ml
1½ pints	851	900 ml
1¾ pints	992	1000 ml (1 litre)

Spoon measures All spoon measures given in this book are level unless otherwise stated.

Can sizes At present, cans are marked with the exact (usually to the nearest whole number) metric equivalent of the Imperial weight of the contents, so we have followed this practice when giving can sizes.

Flour Plain flour is used in the recipes, unless specified otherwise.

Stock Use boiling water poured on to a stock cube.

Notes for American and Australian users

In America the 8-oz measuring cup is used. In Australia metric measures are now used in conjunction with the standard 250-ml measuring cup. The Imperial pint, used in Britain and Australia, is 20 fl oz, while the American pint is 16 fl oz. It is important to remember that the Australian tablespoon differs from both the British and American tablespoons; the table below gives a comparison. The British standard tablespoon, which has been used throughout this book, holds 17·7 ml, the American 14·2 ml, and the Australian 20 ml. A teaspoon holds approximately 5 ml in all three countries.

British	American	Australian
1 teaspoon	1 teaspoon	1 teaspoon
1 tablespoon	1 tablespoon	1 tablespoon
2 tablespoons	3 tablespoons	2 tablespoons
3½ tablespoons	4 tablespoons	3 tablespoons
4 tablespoons	5 tablespoons	3½ tablespoons

An Imperial/American guide to solid and liquid measures

Solid measures

IMPERIAL	AMERICAN
1 lb butter or margarine	2 cups
1 lb flour	4 cups
1 lb granulated or castor sugar	2 cups
1 lb icing sugar	3 cups
8 oz rice	1 cup

Liquid measures

IMPERIAL	AMERICAN
¼ pint liquid	⅔ cup liquid
½ pint	1¼ cups
¾ pint	2 cups
1 pint	2½ cups
1½ pints	3¾ cups
2 pints	5 cups (2½ pints)

Note When making any of the recipes in this book, only follow one set of measures as they are not interchangeable.

American terms

The list below gives some American equivalents or substitutes for terms and ingredients used in this book.

BRITISH/AMERICAN
cling film/saran wrap
greaseproof paper/wax paper
foil/aluminium foil
kitchen paper/paper towels
liquidise/blend
mince/grind
packet/package
polythene/plastic

Introduction

For those embarking on microwave cookery for the first time, I am sure you will find it as exciting and rewarding as I have done. It is a completely different way of cooking, so it is important to read and understand the introductory chapter before launching into the recipes.

All the recipes were created and tested in the Hamlyn test kitchen. I would like to thank Bridget Jones for her invaluable help in compiling these recipes and assistance on the photography sessions. The scope of food that can be cooked in a microwave is endless, as you will discover when you start using it yourself. Even your favourite recipes can be adapted for the microwave. With the busy pace of everyday life, time becomes more valuable to everyone. This is where the microwave oven plays an important role. Once you have mastered the art of microwave cookery, you will never look back!

There are many models of microwave oven available, and new ones are coming on to the market all the time. It is impossible to keep up to date with the latest trends, as the whole concept of microwave cookery is moving very quickly. The expansion of the market is probably due to more working wives leading a very active life. To the next generation of housewives a microwave oven will become as much a necessity as the freezer is to the housewife of today.

I would like also to thank Jenny Webb, a well-known authority on microwave ovens, for her help and advice in compiling this book.

I hope you will enjoy your new adventure into the world of microwave cooking as much as I have done.

All about microwave ovens

Microwave ovens have opened up a whole new concept in cookery. Originally used mainly in the catering industry, their enormous advantages for home use are now being realised. Not only do they save time, by the speed in which foods cook, but the resulting reduction in fuel costs can be considerable.

For the housewife of today, one of the most valuable aspects of the microwave oven must be its ability to cook foods straight from the freezer; no lengthy defrosting time is required—simply transfer the dish from the freezer to the microwave, and the meal is ready in a matter of minutes.

However, before beginning to use the microwave oven it is important to understand exactly how it operates—and how you should operate it to be assured of maximum success.

The microwave oven

All microwave ovens consist of a basic unit with varying levels of power. Some have additional features to the standard model, such as automatic defrosting systems, browning elements, Stay-Hot controls and revolving turntables. In spite of these features the basic principle of microwave cooking remains the same.

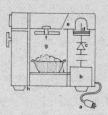

Cross-section of a microwave oven

How the microwave oven works

(a) The *plug* is inserted into the socket and the energy begins to flow.

(b) The *power transformer* increases the voltage and supplies the components in the high voltage circuit.

(c) The high voltage *rectifier and capacitor* changes the alternating voltage to undirectional voltage.

(d) The *magnetron* converts the electrical energy into electromagnetic or microwave energy.

(e) The *waveguide* guides the microwave energy towards the oven cavity.

(f) The *wave stirrer* distributes the microwave evenly throughout the oven.

(g) The *oven cavity* has metallic walls, ceiling and floor which reflect the microwaves.

(h) The *oven door* is fitted with special seals to ensure that there is the minimum of microwave leakage. At least one cut-out device is incorporated in the door so that the microwave energy is automatically switched off when the door is opened.

(i) The *oven shelf* on which the food or container is placed.

How the microwave oven cooks or heats food

Microwaves can react in one of three ways when used with different substances. They are either

(a) reflected or

(b) transmitted *or*

(c) absorbed

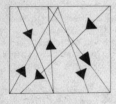
a) reflected

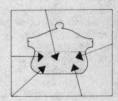
b) transmitted

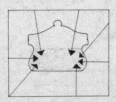
c) absorbed

(a) Microwaves are *reflected* by metal or aluminium foil, just as a mirror will reflect light. The oven cavity is made of metal so that the waves are reflected on to the food. It is therefore important to remember *not to use metal containers* in the oven as

11

the microwaves would be reflected back, avoiding contact with the food.

(b) Microwaves are *transmitted* through substances such as glass, china, ceramics, paper and some plastic, just as light passes through a window. Certain glass containers and plastics should only be used for short time heating, whilst the other types of containers are the most suitable for microwave cooking.

(c) Microwaves are *absorbed* by food and liquid. The microwaves penetrate about 2.5–3.5 cm/1–1½ inches into the food, after which the heat is transferred by conduction.

The microwaves cause the molecules in the food to agitate, producing friction, which creates heat enabling the food to cook quickly.

Safety Factors
All microwave ovens are fitted with safety devices ensuring the minimum of microwave leakage. The door is designed so that the microwave energy cuts off immediately it is opened. Some models are designed with drop-down doors; it is important not to stand heavy dishes on these, or even lean on them, as the alignment could be damaged.

Always remember to switch off the oven at the socket outlet, when not in use. With some ovens, if the control switch is accidentally turned on when the microwave is empty, the magnetron could be damaged.

When cleaning the microwave oven, do not allow the cleaning agent to soil or accumulate around the door seal, as this could prevent a tight seal when the door is closed. Never hang damp tea-towels on the oven door.

Do not attempt to use the oven if it becomes damaged, or try to repair it yourself. Always contact a qualified engineer.

Care and maintenance
Never use an abrasive cleaner to clean the interior of the oven, as it can scratch the metallic walls. Do not use aerosols either, as these may penetrate the internal parts of the oven. Simply wipe over with a cloth wrung out in soapy water and rinse with a clean cloth, or follow the manufacturer's instructions. Any persistent smells can be eliminated by heating a cup of lemon juice and water in the microwave.

Cooking utensils
The range of cooking utensils that can be used in the microwave oven is wide. In fact the choice is probably wider than when cooking in a conventional oven. It is, however, important to remember a few basic rules. *Always avoid metal*

dishes, metal baking trays, stainless steel dishes, foil dishes, cast-iron casseroles, dishes trimmed with metallic designs, dishes that have a certain amount of metal actually in the glaze or composition, glassware saucepans with metal screws or handles, metal ties on frozen foods and foil-lined freezer bags. It is sometimes permissible to use small pieces of aluminium foil to protect wing tips of poultry or any parts of food that may cook more quickly, provided the foil does not come into contact with the oven walls. Always read the manufacturer's instruction booklet first, as individual microwave ovens do vary in exactly what is allowed.

China and pottery dishes
Use any ovenproof dishes or containers that you would normally use in a conventional oven, but if using a pottery dish check that it is not porous. Also remember to avoid using dishes trimmed with a metallic design. If you are using the same dish to cook and serve the food, remember that the dish will become hot as it absorbs heat from the food.

Glassware
Ovenproof glassware such as measuring jugs, basins and mixing bowls are ideal for the microwave, provided there are no metal trims or handles with screws.

Paper
Paper plates, cups, paper kitchen towels and napkins are all suitable for use in the microwave, particularly for reheating purposes and short time cooking. Check plates with a wax coating as they are inclined to melt! Food with a high liquid content, e.g. casseroles, will cause a paper plate to become soggy on reheating. Paper kitchen towels are ideal for cooking fatty foods, e.g. bacon, as they absorb the fat. They are also useful for covering food to prevent any spitting.

Plastics
Only the rigid plastic containers are suitable for the microwave. They should be confined to reheating purposes rather than prolonged cooking. If you are in doubt try a simple test – half-fill a container with water and bring to the boil in the microwave. Check at intervals that the container is still intact.

Plastic wrap
Cling film or freezer film is invaluable for covering dishes. Great care must be taken when removing the film, as trapped steam may cause a burn. It is advisable to pierce the film at intervals before cooking.

Plastic bags
Bags such as boil-in-bags, freezer bags and cook-bags may be used provided there are no metal ties. Use elastic bands or string to secure the bags, but make sure they are loosely tied to allow the steam to escape.

Wooden bowls
These are only suitable for short reheating purposes, e.g. when heating bread rolls.

Microwave accessories

The microwave browning dish
The microwave browning dish helps overcome the problem of browning food in the standard microwave oven. Its primary function is to brown meats, fish and poultry, although it can also be used successfully for cooking eggs and frying sandwiches.

It is a glass-ceramic dish with feet, designed so that the base of the dish does not come into contact with the base of the microwave. The outer side of the base is coated with a special light grey coating which absorbs the microwave energy. The empty dish is preheated in the microwave, the base becomes hot and changes colour. This dish can be used for casseroles, without the pre-heating period, provided the entire base is covered with the food. The pre-heating time of the dish varies according to the type of food being cooked and the output of the oven, so always follow the manufacturer's instructions. Do check that your particular model of microwave oven permits the use of this special dish. Corning Glass International is just one of the companies to manufacture this type of dish.

Microwave browning dish

Microwave / freezer containers
Lakeland Plastics are now producing a range of microwave/freezer containers. These are manufactured from a selection of polythene and polystyrene, with the ability to withstand extreme temperatures, enabling the containers to be used more than once, and to take food in the container straight from the freezer to microwave.

Microwave cooking terms
Stirring

The stirring of food is necessary in some recipes to obtain an even distribution of heat throughout, e.g. casseroles, soups, sauces, etc. As the microwaves cook the exposed outer edges of the food first, stirring helps to distribute the heat more evenly.

When stirring, remove the dish from the oven and stir the contents so that the inside food is moved to the outer edges of the dish, and vice versa.

Stirring food to bring food in
centre to the outer edges

Rearrangement and turning of food.

When it is not possible to stir the food, the food must be rearranged in the microwave, for the same reason. This applies to dishes such as crème caramel, crème brûlée, etc.

If using individual dishes, it is necessary to rearrange the positions during cooking so they can all cook evenly. A large dish, e.g. a cheesecake, will simply require turning during cooking.

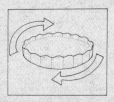

Turning a dish during cooking

Standing time

All food continues to cook to a certain degree once removed from the microwave oven, so it is sometimes necessary to have a standing period, to allow the heat to penetrate to the centre, e.g. a joint of meat. (See chart on page 61). Sometimes the standing time comes in between the cooking times, e.g. a cheesecake requires a standing period as the mixture cannot be stirred, the dish can only be rotated. The standing time allows the heat to transfer naturally into the cooler centre of the food.

With smaller items such as vegetables the time between being removed from the microwave and being served is sufficient for heat transference. The denser the food the longer the standing time.

Defrosting frozen food in the microwave

The freezer and the microwave oven are natural partners. Frozen food can be taken from the freezer and put straight into the microwave oven, provided it is not in a foil container or a freezer bag lined with foil, and all the metal fastenings have been removed.

Defrosting in the standard microwave oven needs more attention than in a microwave with an automatic defrosting system, as the defrosting times and the standing times have to be alternated manually. The standing time allows the heat to be conducted into the centre of the frozen food, without actual cooking taking place. If food was defrosted without standing times, it would be unevenly thawed.

For defrosting times of meat (see page 89), chicken (see page 89), and convenience foods (see pages 169-70).

If you have to transfer a block of frozen food to a different container for defrosting, choose a container to fit the shape of the frozen food. If the dish has too wide a surface area, the outside of the food will defrost, covering the base of the dish, and this will cook while the centre of the food remains frozen.

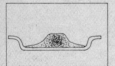 

Frozen food being defrosted in
(left) too large a dish and (right)
correct-sized dish

Factors influencing microwave cooking

Starting temperatures

The colder the food when put into the microwave oven, the longer cooking time is required; so allowances must be made if using food straight from the refrigerator or freezer.

16

Density
The denser the food, the longer it will take to cook.

Shapes
Always aim for uniform shapes, especially with joints of meat. If one end of the joint is much thinner, this will obviously cook more quickly than the denser part of the joint. However, there are some joints which are never uniform, e.g. a leg of lamb. To overcome this problem , it is a good idea to bone and stuff the joint or bone and tie it into a neat shape. If your microwave oven permits the use of foil, then protect the thinner part of the leg with foil, and this will slow down the cooking time on the covered part.

Poultry should always have the legs and wings well tucked into the body. If these protrude then they will cook well in advance of the rest of the bird.

Frozen casseroles are normally an ideal shape to allow even defrosting.

Timing
The timing is probably the most crucial part of microwave cookery and it will often take a while to adjust to it. Each manufacturer provides a guide to timing for their particular model, as the levels of microwave energy vary with the different makes of oven. Always read the instructions carefully.

Remember it is better to undercook than to overcook. Undercooked food can always be rectified, but once overcooked the food becomes dehydrated and cannot be saved.

Unlike conventional cooking, the microwave cooking time increases with any additional items in the oven; for example, two mugs of coffee will take longer than one mug.

Cooking time is also affected by the shape and size of the cooking utensil used. If you are going to use utensils different from those stipulated in the recipes, remember to watch the timing carefully.

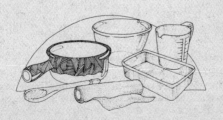

Information
for using the recipes

As microwave ovens have produced a completely new concept in the world of cookery, it is important to read the chapter 'All about microwave ovens' before trying out the microwave-tested recipes in the book. It will make it easier for you to understand and enjoy trying the recipes.

All the recipes in this book were created and tested using a standard microwave oven with an output of 600 watts. Check the output of your oven and adjust the timing accordingly, using the times stated in the recipes as a guide. If your microwave oven has an output higher than 600 watts, the timings are going to be slightly shorter. If the output is below 600 watts, then the cooking time will be longer. In each recipe the size and shape of utensil used has been given, also the total microwave cooking time and number of servings; so all the relevant information is there at a glance.

The utensils used have been kept to basic, everyday equipment usually found in any kitchen; glass measuring jugs, ovenproof mixing bowls, basins and casserole dishes.

If the food requires covering, then it is specified in the recipe. Cling film, freezer film, greaseproof paper and kitchen paper are all suitable. It is worth remembering to go easy on the seasonings, as flavours can become accentuated. The shorter cooking time does not allow the seasoning to be readily absorbed, thus making it more concentrated. When a recipe refers to stock, use boiling water poured onto a stock cube. If the stock is allowed to cool before being used, the cooking time will need to be increased.

And lastly, do refer to the manufacturer's instruction booklet for details about your particular microwave oven.

Soups and starters

Home-made soups are delicious cooked in the microwave. They can be prepared in advance and then reheated in the microwave when required. Always remember that food cooked or reheated in the microwave becomes extremely hot, so allow the soup to cool slightly before serving.

In emergencies canned soups can be reheated actually in the soup bowl, thus reducing washing up! Dried packet soups can be made and cooked in an ovenproof pudding basin.

Pâté is always popular, and is easy to cook in the microwave. Keep it in a refrigerator for up to 3 days or freeze until required.

Spinach soup

Utensil: 2.25-litre /4-pint ovenproof mixing bowl.
Microwave cooking time: 12 minutes

Serves: 4

METRIC/IMPERIAL

25 g/1 oz butter
25 g/1 oz flour
450 ml/¾ pint milk
300 ml/½ pint hot chicken
  stock
½ teaspoon nutmeg

1 tablespoon grated onion
salt and freshly ground black
  pepper
1 (227-g/8-oz) packet frozen
  chopped spinach, thawed
double cream to swirl

Place the butter in the mixing bowl and melt in the microwave for 1 minute. Stir in the flour until well mixed, then gradually add the milk, stock, nutmeg, onion and seasoning, whisking well. Cook in the microwave for 7 minutes, whisking 3 times to prevent lumps forming. Add the spinach and mix well. Cook for a further 4 minutes in the microwave. Allow to cool slightly before liquidising. Reheat in the microwave if necessary. Swirl cream into the soup just before serving.

Bouillabaisse

Utensil: 1.75-litre/3-pint casserole dish
Microwave cooking time: 14 minutes

Serves: 4

METRIC/IMPERIAL

1 tablespoon oil
1 small onion, finely chopped
1 clove garlic, crushed
1 (226-g/8-oz) can tomatoes
900 ml/1½ pints hot stock
¼ teaspoon curry powder
1 tablespoon tomato purée

salt and freshly ground black pepper
2 tablespoons chopped parsley
225 g/8 oz white fish, cut into bite-size pieces
225 g/8 oz peeled prawns
1 (150-g/5¼-oz) can mussels

Place the oil, onion and garlic in the casserole dish and cook in the microwave for 2 minutes. Stir in all the remaining ingredients, except the prawns and mussels, and cook in the microwave for 11 minutes, stirring twice during cooking. Add the prawns and mussels and continue to cook in the microwave for a further 1-2 minutes. Adjust the seasoning and allow to stand for a few minutes before serving.

Sweetcorn soup

Utensil: 2.25-litre/4-pint ovenproof mixing bowl
Microwave cooking time: 8 minutes

Serves: 4

METRIC/IMPERIAL

15 g/½ oz butter
1 medium onion, finely
 chopped
50 g/2 oz bacon, chopped
15 g/½ oz cornflour
300 ml/½ pint milk

2 (170-g/6-oz) packets frozen
 sweetcorn, thawed
300 ml/½ pint hot chicken
 stock
salt and freshly ground black
 pepper

Place the butter, onion and bacon in the mixing bowl and cook in the microwave for 1 minute. Blend the cornflour and milk together and pour on to the bacon and onion. Cook in the microwave for 4 minutes, stirring twice during cooking. Whisk the sauce and add the sweetcorn, reserving a little for garnish, and stock. Return to the microwave for 3 minutes. Allow to cool slightly then liquidise the soup. Adjust the seasoning and reheat in the microwave if necessary. Garnish with reserved sweetcorn.

Cauliflower soup

Utensils: 2.25-litre/4-pint ovenproof mixing bowl,
cook-bag
Microwave cooking time: 16 minutes

Serves : 4

METRIC/IMPERIAL

50 g/2 oz butter
1 onion, finely diced
2 tablespoons flour
750 ml/1¼ pints hot chicken
 stock
1 (339-g/12-oz) packet frozen
 cauliflower florets

salt and freshly ground black
 pepper
Garnish:
2 tablespoons single cream
chopped parsley

Place the butter and onion in the mixing bowl and cook in the microwave for 2 minutes. Stir in the flour, then pour in the stock and return to the microwave for 3 minutes. Place the frozen cauliflower in a cook-bag, secure loosely with an elastic band and cook in the microwave for 9 minutes, turning 3 times. Add the cauliflower florets to the sauce and cook in the microwave for 2 minutes. Allow to cool slightly then liquidise or sieve the soup. Adjust the seasoning and reheat in the microwave if necessary. Just before serving, stir in the cream and chopped parsley.

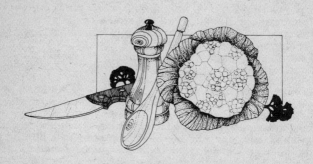

French onion soup

Utensil: 2.25-litre/4-pint ovenproof mixing bowl
Microwave cooking time: 5 minutes

Serves: 4

METRIC /IMPERIAL

50 g/2 oz butter
350 g/12 oz onions, thinly sliced
2 tablespoons flour

generous litre/2 pints hot beef stock
salt and freshly ground black pepper
3 tablespoons sherry

On a conventional cooker, melt the butter in a medium-sized saucepan. Add the onions and cook until brown, then stir in the flour to absorb most of the butter.

Gradually stir in the beef stock and seasoning. Transfer the soup to the mixing bowl. Cook in the microwave for 5 minutes. Stir in the sherry and allow to stand for a few minutes before serving.

Note: In order to obtain a good rich brown colour to this soup, it is necessary to fry the onions initially on the conventional cooker.

Minestrone soup

Utensil: 2.25-litre/4-pint ovenproof mixing bowl
Microwave cooking time: 23 minutes

Serves: 4

METRIC/IMPERIAL

1 tablespoon oil
1 carrot, sliced
1 stick celery, sliced
1 onion, chopped
1 potato, peeled and
  chopped
1 clove garlic, crushed
900 ml/1½ pints hot ham
  stock

25 g/1 oz spaghetti, broken
  into pieces
1 (226-g/8oz) can tomatoes
1 leek, shredded
Garnish:
grated Parmesan cheese
chopped parsley

Place the oil, prepared vegetables and garlic into the mixing
bowl and cook in the microwave for 3 minutes. Stir well and
add the stock and spaghetti, then cook in the microwave for
13 minutes, stirring twice during cooking. Add the tomatoes
and leek and cook for a further 7 minutes in the microwave,
stirring once. Allow to stand for a few minutes before serving.
Garnish with Parmesan and chopped parsley.

Stilton soup

Utensil: 2.25-litre/4 pint ovenproof mixing bowl
Microwave cooking time: 8 minutes

Serves: 4

METRIC/IMPERIAL

1 tablespoon oil
1 small onion, finely
  chopped
1 tablespoon flour
300 ml/½ pint milk
600 ml/1 pint hot chicken
  stock
salt and freshly ground black
  pepper

1 bay leaf
pinch ground mace, nutmeg
  and cayenne pepper
225 g/8 oz Stilton cheese,
  crumbled
150 ml/¼ pint single cream

Place the oil and onion in the mixing bowl and cook in the microwave for 2 minutes. Stir in the flour then add all the remaining ingredients except the Stilton cheese and cream. Cook in the microwave for 5 minutes, stirring once. Add the cheese, reserving a little for garnish. Return to the microwave for 1 minute. Allow to cool slightly then liquidise or sieve the soup. Reheat in the microwave if necessary. Stir in the cream and sprinkle with the reserved Stilton.

Pea soup with bacon meatballs

Utensils: 2.25-litre/4-pint ovenproof mixing bowl,
1.15-litre 2-pint round ovenproof dish
Microwave cooking time: 23 minutes

Serves: 6

METRIC/IMPERIAL

Meatballs:
1 large onion, finely
  chopped
350 g/12 oz smoked streaky
  bacon, derinded and finely
  chopped

75 g/3 oz fresh breadcrumbs
2 teaspoons dried mixed
  herbs
1 egg
salt and freshly ground black
  pepper

Soup:

1 large onion, finely
  chopped
150 g/5 oz potatoes, peeled
  and cut into chunks
50 g/2 oz butter

300 ml/½ pint boiling
  chicken stock made with 2
  stock cubes
1 (454-g/1-lb) packet frozen
  peas

Place the onion and bacon in the mixing bowl and cook in
the microwave for 2 minutes. Add the breadcrumbs, mixed
herbs, egg and seasoning and mix together. With wet hands,
form the mixture into approximately 15 small balls and set
aside.

For the soup, place the onion, potato and butter in the
mixing bowl and cook in the microwave for 6 minutes,
stirring once during cooking. Stir in the chicken stock,
seasoning and frozen peas. Cook in the microwave for a
further 5 minutes, stirring twice during cooking. Allow to
cool slightly, then liquidise the mixture until smooth.
Meanwhile, place half the meatballs on the round dish and
cook in the microwave for 4 minutes, turning the meatballs
over once during cooking. Repeat with the remaining
meatballs. Add another 300 ml/½ pint of boiling water to the
puréed soup and reheat in the microwave for 2 minutes.
Serve the meatballs in the soup.

Smoked sausage chowder

Utensil: 2.25-litre/4-pint ovenproof mixing bowl
Microwave cooking time: 23 minutes

Serves: 6

METRIC/IMPERIAL

25 g/1oz butter
225 g/8 oz pickling onions,
  peeled
4 tablespoons plain flour
300 ml/½ pint boiling
  chicken stock
600 ml/1 pint medium-sweet
  cider
1 teaspoon French mustard

salt and freshly ground black
  pepper
175 g/6 oz Caerphilly
  cheese, crumbled
350 g/12 oz smoked Dutch
  pork sausage, skinned and
  cubed
3 tablespoons chopped fresh
  parsley

Place the butter and onions in the mixing bowl. Cook in the
microwave for 4 minutes. Stir in the flour, then slowly stir in
the chicken stock. Add the cider, mustard, seasoning and

cheese. Cook in the microwave for 4 minutes. Add the sausage and cook in the microwave for a further 15 minutes, stirring twice during cooking. Stir in the chopped parsley before serving with hot French bread.

Lemon soup with prawns

Utensil: 1-litre/1¾-pint glass measuring jug
Microwave cooking time: 8 minutes

Serves: 6

METRIC/IMPERIAL

1 large onion, finely
  chopped
rind and juice of 2 lemons
50 g/2 oz butter
2 level tablespoons plain
  flour
1 tablespoon clear honey
salt and freshly ground black
  pepper

150ml/¼ pint boiling
  chicken stock
150 ml/¼ pint dry sherry
1 tablespoon chopped fresh
  or ½ tablespoon dried
  tarragon
Garnish:
175 g/6 oz peeled prawns
150 ml/¼ pint soured cream

Place the onion, lemon rind and butter in the jug. Cook in the microwave for 2 minutes. Add the flour and stir well. Stir in the lemon juice, honey, seasoning, chicken stock and enough boiling water to give 600 ml/1 pint of liquid. Cook in the microwave for 4 minutes, stirring once during cooking. Stir in the sherry, tarragon and enough extra boiling water to make the liquid up to 900 ml/1½ pints. Cook in the microwave for a further 2 minutes. Mix together the prawns and soured cream and season lightly. Pour the soup into serving dishes and divide the garnish between them.

Lentil and bacon soup

Utensil: 2.25-litre/4-pint ovenproof mixing bowl
Microwave cooking time: 13 minutes

Serves: 4

METRIC/IMPERIAL

100 g/4oz lentils
900 ml/1½ pints hot ham
  stock
4 rashers lean bacon,
  chopped
1 onion, finely chopped

2 sticks celery, chopped
salt and freshly ground black
  pepper
pinch cayenne pepper
2 tablespoons chopped
  parsley

Soak the lentils overnight and then drain. Place the stock,
bacon, onion, celery, seasoning and drained lentils in the
ovenproof mixing bowl and cook in the microwave for 13
minutes, stirring twice during cooking. Allow to cool slightly
then liquidise or sieve the soup. Adjust the seasoning and stir
in the chopped parsley, reheat in the microwave if necessary.

Broccoli soup

Utensil: 1.5-litre/2½-pint round ovenproof dish
Microwave cooking time: 8½-9 minutes

Serves : 4

METRIC/IMPERIAL

1 small onion, finely
  chopped
25 g/1oz butter
25 g/1 oz flour
600 ml/1 pint hot chicken
  stock

1 (226-g/8-oz) packet frozen
  broccoli, thawed and
  roughly chopped
salt and freshly ground black
  pepper
pinch freshly ground nutmeg
300 ml/½ pint milk

Place the onion and butter in the round dish and cook in the
microwave for 2 minutes. Stir in the flour, then add the stock,
chopped broccoli, reserving a little for the garnish, and
seasonings. Cook in the microwave for 6 minutes, stirring
twice during cooking. Allow to cool slightly then liquidise or
sieve the soup. Adjust the seasoning and pour in the milk.
Reheat in the microwave for ½-1 minute. Allow to stand a

few minutes before serving. Garnish with the reserved broccoli.

Leek and potato soup

Utensils: cook-bag, 1-litre/2-pint ovenproof pudding basin, 2.25-litre/4-pint ovenproof mixing bowl
Microwave cooking time: 16 minutes

Serves: 4

METRIC/IMPERIAL

450 g/1 lb leeks, washed and sliced
2 medium potatoes, peeled and diced
750 ml/1¼ pints milk

1 chicken stock cube
150 ml/¼ pint boiling water
salt and freshly ground black pepper

Place the leeks and potatoes together in a cook-bag. Seal loosely with an elastic band or freezer tape and cook in the microwave for 10 minutes.

Heat the milk in the pudding basin in the microwave for 3 minutes and add to the leeks and potatoes in the mixing bowl. Stir in the stock cube and boiling water. Cook in the microwave for 3 minutes, cool slightly before liquidising or sieving the soup. Season to taste. Reheat in the microwave if necessary.

Creamy onion soup

**Utensils: 3-5 litre/6-pint ovenproof mixing bowl,
300-ml/½-pint glass measuring jug
Microwave cooking time: 16 minutes**

Serves: 4

METRIC/IMPERIAL

25 g/1 oz butter
450 g/1 lb onions, chopped
1 tablespoon flour
600 ml/1 pint hot chicken
  stock

salt and freshly ground black
  pepper
1 tablespoon chopped
  parsley
300 ml/½ pint milk

Place the butter in the mixing bowl and melt in the
microwave for 1 minute. Add the onions and cook in the
microwave for a further 3 minutes. Stir in the flour then
carefully mix in the chicken stock, seasoning and parsley,
return to the microwave for 10 minutes.

Heat the milk in the measuring jug in the microwave for 2
minutes and add to the soup. Sieve or liquidise; reheat if
necessary in the microwave oven and serve.

Tomato and horseradish soup

Utensil: 2.25-litre/4-pint ovenproof mixing bowl
Microwave cooking time: 13 minutes

Serves: 4

METRIC/IMPERIAL

25 g/1 oz butter
100 g/4 oz onion, finely
  chopped
25 g/1 oz flour
450 g/1 lb tomatoes, skinned
  and chopped
600 ml/1 pint hot chicken
  stock
salt and freshly ground black
  pepper

3 teaspoons creamed
  horseradish
3 tablespoons tomato purée
pinch ground mace
Garnish:
4 tablespoons double cream
1 teaspoon creamed
  horseradish

Place the butter in the mixing bowl and melt in the
microwave for 1 minute. Add the onion and cook for 2
minutes. Stir in the flour and tomatoes, gradually add the
chicken stock, seasoning, creamed horseradish, tomato purée
and mace. Cook in the microwave for 10 minutes. Allow to
cool slightly then sieve or liquidise. Garnish with swirls of
double cream mixed with the creamed horseradish.

Summer soup

**Utensils: cook-bag, 3.5-litre/6-pint ovenproof
mixing bowl, 600-ml/1-pint glass measuring jug
Microwave cooking time: 15 minutes**

Serves: 4

METRIC/IMPERIAL

*225 g/8 oz potatoes, diced
50 g/2 oz onion, chopped
300 ml/½ pint hot chicken
  stock
1 lettuce, shredded
salt and freshly ground black
  pepper*

*pinch ground mace
600 ml/1 pint milk
Garnish:
4 tablespoons double cream
chopped mint*

Place the potatoes, onion and stock in the cook-bag and seal
loosely with an elastic band or freezer tape. Cook in the
microwave for 5 minutes then place in the mixing bowl. Add
the lettuce and seasonings to the potato mixture.

Heat the milk in the measuring jug in the microwave for 3
minutes then add to the soup and continue to cook in the
microwave for 7 minutes. Liquidise or sieve the soup and
serve hot or cold. Swirl the cream on top and sprinkle with
chopped mint.

Artichoke soup

Utensils: cook-bag, 2.25-litre/4-pint mixing bowl,
300-ml/½-pint glass measuring jug
Microwave cooking time: 19 minutes

Serves: 4

METRIC/IMPERIAL

450 g/1 lb Jerusalem
  artichokes, peeled and
  sliced
1 small onion, finely
  chopped
2 tablespoons lemon juice
25 g/1 oz butter

2 tablespoons flour
600 ml/1 pint hot chicken
  stock
300 ml/½ pint milk
salt and freshly ground black
  pepper

Place the artichokes, onion, lemon juice and butter in the
cook-bag. Seal loosely with an elastic band or freezer tape
and cook in the microwave for 8 minutes.

Turn the artichoke mixture into the mixing bowl and stir in
the flour. Carefully stir in the stock and cook in the
microwave for 9 minutes, stirring 4 times during cooking.

Allow to cool slightly then liquidise or sieve the soup. Heat
the milk in the measuring jug in the microwave for 2 minutes
and stir into the soup. Taste and season the soup before
serving.

Chicken liver pâté

Utensils: 1.5-litre/2½-pint round ovenproof dish.
600-ml/1-pint glass measuring jug
Microwave cooking time: 8 minutes

Serves: 4

METRIC/IMPERIAL

25 g/1 oz butter
1 tablespoon oil
1 clove garlic, crushed
1 medium onion, finely
  chopped
350 g/12 oz chicken livers,
  washed and dried
salt and freshly ground black
  pepper

freshly ground nutmeg
1 tablespoon brandy
100 g/4 oz butter
Garnish:
lemon slices
cress

Place the butter, oil, garlic and onion in the dish and cook in the microwave for 3 minutes, stirring once during cooking. Add the chicken livers and seasonings, continue to cook in the microwave for 4 minutes, stirring twice. Stir in the brandy, cool slightly and liquidise until smooth. Place in 4 ramekin dishes and smooth the tops.

Place the butter in the jug and melt in the microwave for 1 minute or until melted. Pour over the individual pâtés and place a lemon slice in the butter. Chill until set and garnish with cress.

Farmhouse terrine

Utensils: 20-cm/8-inch round ovenproof pie dish,
0.75-litre/1-1¼-pint ovenproof soufflé dish
Microwave cooking time: 15 minutes

Serves: 4

METRIC/IMPERIAL

100 g/4 oz ox kidney, chopped	*5 rashers streaky bacon, derinded*
225 g/8 oz lamb's liver, chopped	*2 bay leaves*
225 g/8 oz lean pork, chopped	*50 g/2 oz fresh breadcrumbs*
1 small onion, finely chopped	*salt and freshly ground black pepper*
	pinch basil
	1 clove garlic, crushed
	1 egg, beaten

Place the chopped offal, meat and onion in the pie dish and cook in the microwave for 5 minutes, stirring once during cooking. Stretch the bacon rashers using the back of a knife. Place the bay leaves on the base of the soufflé dish. Line the dish with the bacon rashers.

Mix the meats with the remaining ingredients and place in the lined dish, smoothing the surface with a knife. Cover with cling film or greaseproof paper and cook in the microwave for 10 minutes. Allow to stand for 5 minutes. Cover with a clean piece of greaseproof paper and place a heavy weight on a saucer or small plate on top. Allow to cool then refrigerate overnight. Turn out carefully. Serve with French bread and a salad.

Asparagus mousse

Utensil: 600-ml/1-pint glass measuring jug
Microwave cooking time: 2–2½ minutes

Serves: 4–6

METRIC/IMPERIAL

1 (340-g/12-oz) can green
  asparagus spears
15 g/½ oz softened butter
15 g/½ oz flour
2 eggs, separated
15 g/½ oz gelatine
150 ml/¼ pint chicken stock
salt and freshly ground black
  pepper

pinch cayenne pepper
1 teaspoon lemon juice
150 ml/¼ pint double
  cream, whipped
Garnish:
lemon slices
cucumber slices

Drain the juice from the asparagus into the measuring jug
and combine with the butter and flour. Cook in the
microwave for 2–2½ minutes, whisking once during cooking.
Remove from the microwave and whisk well to remove any
lumps. Allow to cool slightly then stir in the egg yolks.

Using the conventional cooker, dissolve the gelatine in the
chicken stock in a saucepan over a low heat. Stir into the
sauce. Chop the asparagus and stir into the sauce with
seasonings and lemon juice. When on the point of setting,
whisk the egg whites and fold into the sauce with the
whipped cream. Pour into a wetted 1-litre/2-pint mould. Chill
until set.

When required, dip the mould quickly into hot water and
turn out. Garnish with lemon and cucumber slices.

Egg mousse

Utensil: 2.25-litre/4-pint ovenproof mixing bowl
Microwave cooking time: 5 minutes

Serves: 4

METRIC/IMPERIAL

25 g/1 oz butter	15 g/½ oz gelatine
1 clove garlic, crushed	2 tablespoons hot water
3 tablespoons flour	Garnish:
300 ml/½ pint milk	quartered hard-boiled eggs
4 hard-boiled eggs, chopped	watercress sprigs
2 eggs, separated	

Melt the butter in the mixing bowl in the microwave for 1
minute. Add the garlic and stir in the flour. Gradually add
the milk, whisking well, and return to the microwave for 4
minutes. Whisk the sauce 4 times during cooking and again
very well at the end of the cooking time.

Add the chopped hard-boiled eggs and egg yolks to the
sauce and cool slightly. Dissolve the gelatine in the hot
water, add to the sauce and leave in a cool place until half
set. Whisk the egg whites until they form stiff peaks then fold
into the half set mixture. Pour into a lightly oiled 1.5-
litre/2½-pint mould and leave to set in a cool place.

Turn out on to a suitable serving dish and garnish with
quartered hard-boiled eggs and sprigs of watercress.

Serve with Melba toast.

Smoked haddock pâté

Utensil: 1.75-litre/3-pint round casserole dish
Microwave cooking time: 5 minutes

Serves: 4

METRIC/IMPERIAL

450 g/1 lb smoked haddock fillets, skinned	salt and freshly ground black pepper
2 tablespoons finely chopped onion	Garnish:
225 g/8 oz cream cheese	lemon wedges
	parsley

Cut the fish into chunks and place in the casserole dish
together with the onion. Cook in the microwave for 5
minutes, stirring twice.

Cool and liquidise the fish with the cream cheese. Taste
and season before pressing into individual ramekin dishes or
a large serving dish. Chill until firm and garnish before serving.

Grapefruit with vermouth

Utensil: kitchen paper
Microwave cooking time: 2 minutes

Serves: 4

METRIC/IMPERIAL

2 tablespoons white
vermouth
2 tablespoons clear honey

2 grapefruit
Garnish:
mint leaf

Mix together the vermouth and honey. Halve the grapefruit
and loosen the segments then carefully spoon the vermouth
mixture over them.

Heat two halves at a time in the microwave on a double
thickness of kitchen paper, allowing 1 minute for each pair.
Half turn the grapefruit after 30 seconds. Serve hot garnished
with a mint leaf.

Smoked mackerel crumble

**Utensils: 4 (11-cm/4½-inch) individual ovenproof
quiche dishes, 1-litre/2-pint ovenproof pudding
basin
Microwave cooking time: 6 minutes**

Serves: 4

METRIC/IMPERIAL

100 g/4 oz smoked mackerel
fillets, skinned
2 tablespoons roughly
chopped onion
2 eggs
150 ml/¼ pint milk
50 g/2 oz Double Gloucester
cheese, grated

1 tablespoon chopped fresh
mixed herbs
75 g/3 oz crunchy peanut
butter
100 g/4 oz crisps and
savoury biscuits, crushed
Garnish:
lemon slices
parsley sprigs

Liquidise the mackerel, onion, eggs, milk and cheese together. Stir in the herbs and divide the mixture between the 4 quiche dishes. Cook two at a time in the microwave allowing each pair 2 minutes.

Melt the peanut butter in the pudding basin in the microwave for 2 minutes then add the crumbs and mix well. Top the cooked fish with the crumb mixture and garnish with the lemon slices and parsley sprigs before serving.

Tomato and tuna fish pots

Utensils: 600-ml/1-pint ovenproof pudding basin, 4
150-ml/¼-pint ovenproof ramekin dishes
Microwave cooking time: 3½ minutes

Serves: 4

METRIC/IMPERIAL

1 small onion, chopped
25 g/1 oz butter
2 cloves garlic, crushed
1 (198-g/7-oz) can tuna fish, flaked
3 tomatoes peeled and chopped

salt and freshly ground black pepper
75 g/3 oz Caerphilly cheese, cut into four slices
Garnish:
50 g/2 oz black olives, stoned and chopped
25 g/1 oz salted crisps, crushed

Place the onion and butter in the pudding basin and cook in the microwave for 2 minutes. Add the garlic, tuna fish, tomatoes and seasoning and mix well. Divide the mixture between the ramekin dishes. Place a slice of cheese on top of each and cook in the microwave for 1½ minutes, turning once during cooking. For the garnish, mix together the black olives and crisps and sprinkle over the top of the cheese. Serve immediately.

Coquilles Saint Jacques

**Utensils: 1-litre/2-pint round ovenproof dish,
600-ml/1-pint glass measuring jug
Microwave cooking time: 8½–9½ minutes**

Serves: 2

METRIC/IMPERIAL

*15 g/½ oz butter
1 small onion, finely
  chopped
100 g/4 oz button
  mushrooms, sliced
150 ml/¼ pint dry white
  wine
4 scallops, washed and
  quartered
1 teaspoon lemon juice
2 tablespoons chopped
  parsley*

*salt and freshly ground black
  pepper
bay leaf
15 g/½ oz butter
15 g/½ oz flour
3 tablespoons single cream
  or milk
2 tablespoons dried
  breadcrumbs
Garnish:
lemon wedges
parsley sprigs*

Place the butter and onion in the dish and cook in the
microwave for 3 minutes. Stir in the mushrooms, wine,
scallops, lemon juice, parsley, seasoning and bay leaf. Cook
in the microwave for 4 minutes, stirring once. Remove and
discard the bay leaf.

Place the butter in the measuring jug and melt in the
microwave for 30-seconds. Stir in the flour and mix into a
smooth paste. Strain the liquor from the scallops on to the
butter and flour mixture together with the cream and stir
well. Pour this sauce on to the scallops and place in 2
scallop shells or individual dishes. Sprinkle with
breadcrumbs and return to the microwave for 1–2 minutes.
Garnish with lemon wedges and parsley sprigs.

Baked avocado with shrimps

Utensil: 600-ml/1-pint glass measuring jug
Microwave cooking time: 3½ minutes

Serves: 4

METRIC/IMPERIAL

150 ml/¼ pint milk
7 g/¼ oz butter
1 tablespoon flour
½ (212-g/7½-oz) can
  shrimps, drained
pinch cayenne pepper
salt and freshly ground black
  pepper

few drops lemon juice
2 teaspoons tomato purée
2 ripe avocado pears
Topping:
1–2 tablespoons fresh
  breadcrumbs

Place the milk in the measuring jug and heat in the
microwave for 30 seconds. Mix the butter with the flour then
whisk gradually into the milk. Return to the microwave for 1
minute, or until thickened. Add the shrimps, cayenne pepper,
seasoning, lemon juice and tomato purée.

Cut the avocado pears in half and remove the stones.
Brush the cut surface with a little lemon juice to prevent
discoloration. Pile the shrimp filling in the centre of each
avocado and sprinkle with breadcrumbs. Place the avocado
pear halves in a circle on a sheet of kitchen paper and return
to the microwave for 2 minutes, stopping after 1 minute to
alter the position of the avocado halves.

Cheese-baked pears

Utensils: 600-ml/1-pint ovenproof pudding basin,
600-ml/1-pint round shallow pie dish
Microwave cooking time: 3½ minutes

Serves: 4

METRIC/IMPERIAL

50 g/2 oz smoked streaky
  bacon, derinded and
  chopped
40 g/1½ oz Cheddar cheese,
  grated
25 g/1 oz fresh breadcrumbs
salt and freshly ground black
  pepper

1 teaspoon French mustard
juice of 1 lemon
2 ripe pears, peeled
25 g/1 oz walnuts, chopped
1 teaspoon dried chives
Garnish:
1 small lettuce
lemon twists

Place the bacon in the pudding basin and cook in the
microwave for 1 minute. Add the cheese, breadcrumbs,
seasoning, mustard and 1 teaspoon of the lemon juice. Mix
well and form into 4 small balls with wet hands. Halve and
core the pears and sprinkle with the remaining lemon juice.
Place the pears flat side up in the pie dish and place a ball
of filling on each half where the core should be. Cook in the
microwave for 2 minutes, turning once during cooking. Mix
the walnuts with the chives and press on top of the cheese
mixture. Cook in the microwave for a further 30 seconds.
Serve on crisp lettuce leaves garnished with twists of lemon.

Note: This recipe is also delicious made with fresh peaches
or canned peach halves. Fresh peaches should be peeled,
halved and stoned whilst canned peaches should be
thoroughly drained before use.

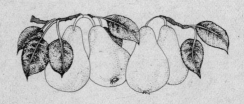

Fish dishes

Fish cooked in the microwave retains all its natural flavour and nutrients. Cook-bags have proved very successful for cooking fish, especially whole fish such as trout.

If you are cooking a large piece of fish, try and arrange it into a uniform shape by tucking any thin parts, such as the tail, underneath. This will prevent the thinner parts overcooking.

Be careful not to overcook fish as it will toughen and dry out. Always undercook slightly, as the fish will continue to cook in its own heat, once removed from the oven.

Soused mackerel

Utensil: 2.25-litre/4-pint deep oblong casserole dish
Microwave cooking time: 16 minutes

Serves: 4

METRIC/IMPERIAL

100 g/4 oz onion, sliced
150 ml/¼ pint vinegar
150 ml/¼ pint water
2 bay leaves
¼ teaspoon salt
freshly ground black pepper

4 mackerel, cleaned and
  boned
Garnish:
lemon wedges
watercress

Place the onion in the casserole dish and pour over the vinegar and water. Add the bay leaves, salt and freshly ground black pepper.

Place 2 mackerel in the liquid and cook in the microwave for 8 minutes, turning the fish 4 times during cooking. Remove the fish from the cooking liquid and cook the second pair of mackerel for approximately 8 minutes. (The second pair of fish may not take quite as long as the first pair since the cooking liquid will have already been heated.) Serve the fish cold, garnished with lemon wedges and watercress.

Lemon-stuffed mackerel

**Utensils: 600-ml/1-pint ovenproof pudding basin,
3.5-litre/6-pint shallow oval ovenproof dish
Microwave cooking time: 26 minutes**

Serves: 4

METRIC/IMPERIAL

1 (225-g/8-oz) cooking
  apple, peeled and cored
1 large onion, chopped
25 g/1 oz butter
grated rind and juice of 1
  lemon
50 g/2 oz fresh white
  breadcrumbs

2 teaspoons dried marjoram
salt and freshly ground black
  pepper
4 mackerel, about 175 g/
  6 oz each, gutted
Garnish:
watercress sprigs
lemon wedges

Finely chop the apple and place in the basin with the onion
and butter. Cook in the microwave for 2 minutes stirring
once during cooking. Add the lemon rind and juice,
breadcrumbs and marjoram. Season to taste and mix
thoroughly.

Rinse the mackerel and divide the filling between the fish,
pressing it well into the body cavity. Place two fish in the
oval dish and cook in the microwave for 12 minutes, turning
the dish 4 times during cooking. Place on a warmed serving
dish and cover with foil. Repeat with the remaining fish.
Garnish with watercress sprigs and wedges of lemon for
serving.

Creamed mackerel with horseradish

Utensils: 1-litre/2-pint ovenproof pudding basin,
cook-bag, piping bag and large star nozzle
Microwave cooking time: 18 minutes

Serves: 4

METRIC/IMPERIAL

1 large onion, chopped	3 tablespoons grated
25 g/1 oz butter	horseradish
450 g/1 lb smoked mackerel	1 kg/2 lb potatoes, peeled
fillets	50 g/2 oz butter
2 tablespoons flour	2 tablespoons water
salt and freshly ground black	Garnish:
pepper	1 tablespoon chopped
300 ml/½ pint milk	parsley

Place the onion in the basin with the butter and cook in the
microwave for 2 minutes stirring once during cooking.

Remove the skin from the fish and flake, discarding any
bones. Add the flour to the onion stirring well. Season
generously, then stir in the milk. Cook in the microwave for 2
minutes. Stir in the horseradish and cook for a further 1
minute. Stir in the flaked fish.

Cut the potatoes into large dice and place in the cook-bag
together with the butter and water. Secure the end loosely
with an elastic band and cook in the microwave for 10
minutes. Turn into a large bowl and season generously. Mash
until smooth. Place the potato in a piping bag fitted with a
large star nozzle and pipe a ring of potato around the edge
of the flan dish. Spoon the fish mixture into the middle of the
dish and cook in the microwave for 3 minutes. Serve
sprinkled with a little chopped parsley.

Kedgeree

Utensils: 1.5-litre/2½-pint shallow oblong
ovenproof dish, 1.75-litre/3-pint round casserole
dish
Microwave cooking time: 22 minutes

Serves: 4

METRIC/IMPERIAL

450 g/1 lb smoked haddock
  fillets
1 tablespoon lemon juice
600 ml/1 pint boiling water
2 tablespoons chopped
  parsley
25 g/1 oz butter
1 onion, finely chopped

175 g/6 oz long grain rice
1 bay leaf
3 hard-boiled eggs, chopped
salt and freshly ground black
  pepper
Garnish:
chopped parsley
lemon slices

Place the fish in the oblong dish together with the lemon
juice, boiling water and parsley. Cook in the microwave for 4
minutes, turning the dish once. Remove the fish and reserve
the stock. Skin and flake the fish, removing any bones.

Heat the butter in the casserole dish in the microwave for
1 minute then add the onion and cook in the microwave for 2
minutes. Add the rice and bay leaf; pour over the fish stock
and cook in the microwave for a further 15 minutes or until
the liquid is absorbed.

Remove the bay leaf then mix in the fish and hard-boiled
eggs. Season with salt and freshly ground black pepper.
Garnish with parsley and lemon slices.

Smoked haddock with creamy prawns

Utensils: 1.75-litre/3-pint shallow oblong
ovenproof dish, 1-litre/2-pint ovenproof pudding
basin
Microwave cooking time: 7 minutes

Serves: 4

METRIC/IMPERIAL

4 smoked haddock fillets,
  about 100 g/4 oz each
4 eggs
3 tablespoons double cream
salt and freshly ground black
  pepper

25 g/1 oz butter
225 g/8 oz peeled prawns
Garnish:
lemon wedges

Place the haddock in the dish and cook in the microwave for 4 minutes turning the dish twice during cooking.

Beat the eggs in the pudding basin with the cream and seasoning. Add the butter and cook in the microwave for 3 minutes, whisking at intervals of 30 seconds, until creamy. Stir in the prawns and arrange over the haddock. Serve immediately, garnished with wedges of lemon.

Paupiettes of plaice in wine sauce

Utensils: 1-litre/2-pint round shallow ovenproof dish, 1-litre/2-pint ovenproof basin
Microwave cooking time: 7 minutes

Serves: 4

METRIC/IMPERIAL

8 plaice fillets, skinned	slice lemon
150 ml/¼ pint white wine	few drops lemon juice
150 ml/¼ pint chicken stock	15 g/½ oz butter
bay leaf	15 g/½ oz flour
blade mace	Garnish:
few peppercorns	few white grapes
salt and freshly ground black pepper	watercress
	croûtons

Roll the plaice fillets and secure with a wooden cocktail stick if necessary. Place the fish in the shallow dish and pour over the wine , stock, bay leaf, blade mace, few peppercorns, salt and pepper, lemon slice and juice. Cover with greaseproof paper and cook in the microwave for 5 minutes, turning the dish once during cooking. Carefully drain off the liquor and reserve. Keep the fish hot.

Mix the butter and flour together in the basin and pour the strained liquor over, whisking well. Cook in the microwave for 1 minute, stir and cook for a further minute. Pour over the plaice and garnish with grapes, watercress and croûtons.

Seafood curry

Utensil: 1.5-litre/2½-pint ovenproof soufflé
dish
Microwave cooking time: 11 minutes

Serves: 4

METRIC/IMPERIAL

1 tablespoon oil
1 medium onion, chopped
2 tablespoons curry powder
2 tablespoons flour
300 ml/½ pint water
225 g/8 oz cod, skinned and
   cut into chunks

50 g/2 oz button mushrooms,
   sliced
salt and freshly ground black
   pepper
150 ml/¼ pint soured cream
225 g/8 oz peeled prawns

Heat the oil in the soufflé dish in the microwave for 2
minutes. Add the onion and curry powder, stir well and cook
in the microwave for 4 minutes. Add the flour and carefully
stir in the water. Add the cod and mushrooms, mix well and
season lightly. Cook for a further 4 minutes in the microwave,
stirring every minute. Stir in the soured cream and prawns
and heat in the microwave for 1 minute before serving with
boiled rice.

Savoury fish crumble

Utensil: 1.75-litre/3-pint round casserole dish
Microwave cooking time: 13 minutes

Serves: 4

METRIC/IMPERIAL

50 g/2 oz butter
1 medium onion, chopped
1 tablespoon chopped green
   pepper
450 g/1 lb cod fillet, skinned
   and boned
salt and freshly ground black
   pepper

75 g/3 oz fresh brown
   breadcrumbs
grated rind of 1 lemon
50 g/2 oz red Leicester
   cheese, grated
2 tablespoons chopped
   parsley

Place the butter in the casserole dish and melt in the microwave for 1 minute. Add the onion and green pepper and cook in the microwave for 4 minutes, stirring twice. Add the flaked fish and season lightly. Cook in the microwave for a further 4 minutes, stirring every minute.

Mix together the remaining ingredients and cover the fish with the mixture. Heat in the microwave for 4 minutes, turning the dish twice.

Baked cod with orange and walnut topping

Utensil: 1.5-litre/2½-pint shallow oblong casserole dish
Microwave cooking time: 10 minutes

Serves: 4

METRIC/IMPERIAL

25 g/1 oz butter
50 g/2 oz onion, chopped
450 g/1 lb cod fillet, skinned
salt and freshly ground black
  pepper
juice and grated rind of 1
  orange

25 g/1 oz fresh brown
  breadcrumbs
50 g/2 oz walnuts, roughly
  chopped
Garnish:
orange segments
bunch watercress

Melt the butter in the casserole dish in the microwave for 1 minute. Add the onion and cook in the microwave for a further 3 minutes. Place the fish in the dish, season lightly and pour over the orange juice. Cook in the microwave for 4 minutes, turning the fish once.

Mix together the orange rind, breadcrumbs and walnuts. Season lightly and place on top of the fish. Heat in the microwave for 2 minutes. Garnish with orange segments and watercress before serving.

Cod with orange pimiento sauce

Utensils: 600-ml/1-pint glass measuring jug. 1.75-litre/3-pint shallow oblong ovenproof dish
Microwave cooking time: 15 minutes

Serves: 4

METRIC/IMPERIAL

1 large onion, finely chopped	1 tablespoon soft brown sugar
50 g/2 oz butter	150 ml/¼ pint boiling water
grated rind and juice of 1 orange	4 cod steaks, about 175 g/6 oz each
1 (190-g/6¾-oz) can pimientos, drained and chopped	salt and freshly ground black pepper
1 tablespoon tomato purée	Garnish:
½ chicken stock cube	1 tablespoon grated Parmesan cheese

Place the onion, butter and orange rind in the jug and cook in the microwave for 2 minutes. Add the pimientos, tomato purée, stock cube, brown sugar, boiling water and orange juice. Stir well and cook in the microwave for 3 minutes. Liquidise until smooth and return to the jug.

Arrange the fish on the oblong dish, season lightly and cook in the microwave for 8 minutes, turning the dish 4 times during cooking. Reheat the sauce for 2 minutes. Serve the fish with the sauce poured over.

Sprinkle the top with a little Parmesan cheese.

Cod provençal

Utensil: 1.5-litre/2½-pint oval ovenproof pie dish
Microwave cooking time: 6 minutes

Serves: 4

METRIC/IMPERIAL

450 g/1 lb cod, cubed	salt and freshly ground black pepper
1 tablespoon oil	pinch basil
1 medium onion, finely chopped	4 tablespoons stuffed olives, sliced
1 clove garlic, crushed	150 ml/¼ pint double cream
2 tomatoes, skinned and sliced	Garnish:
	chopped parsley

Place the cod, oil, onion and garlic in the pie dish. Cover and cook in the microwave for 3 minutes, stirring twice during cooking. Stir in the tomatoes, seasoning, basil and olives, cover and cook in the microwave for a further 2 minutes. Pour over the cream and heat in the microwave for 1 minute. Sprinkle with chopped parsley and serve.

Buttered cod with mushrooms

Utensils: 2.25-litre/4-pint oblong deep ovenproof
dish, 300-ml/½-pint glass measuring jug
Microwave cooking time: 6½ minutes

Serves: 4

METRIC/IMPERIAL

350 g/12 oz cod fillet	75 g/3 oz butter
225 g/8 oz small button mushrooms	grated rind of 1 large lemon
	8 thin slices French bread
salt and freshly ground black pepper	1 tablespoon chopped parsley
1 small clove garlic, crushed	

Skin the fish and cut it into bite-sized chunks, removing any bones. Place in the oblong dish with the mushrooms and season generously. Sprinkle over the garlic and dot with 25g/ 1 oz of butter. Cook in the microwave for 5 minutes, stirring twice during cooking.

Place the remaining butter with the lemon rind in the measuring jug and heat in the microwave for 1½ minutes. Arrange the French bread around the edge of a serving dish and pour over the melted butter.

Spoon the fish mixture into the middle and sprinkle with chopped parsley. Serve immediately.

Devilled crab

Utensil: 900-ml/1½-pint ovenproof basin
Microwave cooking time: 4–5 minutes

Serves: 2

METRIC/IMPERIAL

15 g/½ oz butter
1 small shallot, finely
  chopped
150 g/5 oz crabmeat
1 tablespoon dry sherry
2 tablespoons fresh
  breadcrumbs
pinch cayenne pepper
few drops Worcestershire
  sauce
1 teaspoon Dijon mustard
salt and freshly ground black
  pepper

Topping:
1 tablespoon fresh
  breadcrumbs
1 tablespoon grated
  Parmesan cheese
1 tablespoon chopped
  parsley
Garnish:
lemon slices
watercress sprigs

Place the butter and shallot in the basin and cook in the
microwave for 3 minutes. Stir in the remaining ingredients
until well combined. Divide the mixture between 2 scallop
shells. Mix the topping ingredients and sprinkle over the
devilled crab. Return to the microwave and heat for 1–2
minutes, until hot. Garnish with lemon slices and watercress
sprigs. Serve with hot crusty bread.

Fish and mussel casserole with cider

**Utensils: cook-bag, 1.5-litre/2½-pint oval
ovenproof dish, 600-ml/1-pint glass measuring jug
Microwave cooking time: 11–12 minutes**

Serves: 4

METRIC/IMPERIAL

1 tablespoon oil
1 onion, finely chopped
½ red pepper, finely sliced
1 small aubergine, finely
  sliced
few drops lemon juice
450 g/1 lb cod or haddock,
  cut into bite-size pieces
1 (150-g/5¼-oz) can mussels,
  drained
300 ml/½ pint dry cider

salt and freshly ground black
  pepper
1 teaspoon fresh marjoram
2 tablespoons chopped
  parsley
25 g/1 oz butter
25 g/1 oz flour
Garnish:
lemon slices
watercress

Place the oil, onion, pepper and aubergine in the cook-bag,
secure loosely with an elastic band and cook in the
microwave for 4 minutes, rearranging the vegetables half
way through the cooking time. Carefully transfer to the oval
dish and add the lemon juice, fish, mussels, cider, seasoning
and herbs. Cover with cling film and cook in the microwave
for 5 minutes, stirring once.

    Allow to stand for 2 minutes. Place the butter and flour in
the measuring jug and mix well together. Strain the fish
liquor into the jug, stirring well. Cook in the microwave for
2–3 minutes until thickened. Pour over the fish and reheat in
the microwave if necessary. Garnish with lemon slices and
watercress.

Stuffed herrings

Utensils: 1-litre/2-pint ovenproof pudding basin, 1-litre/2-pint shallow pie dish
Microwave cooking time: 10 minutes

Serves: 4

METRIC/IMPERIAL

25 g/1 oz butter
50 g/2 oz onion, finely chopped
100 g/4 oz cooking apple, chopped
juice of ½ lemon
½ teaspoon dry mustard
50 g/2 oz fresh white breadcrumbs

½ teaspoon dried rosemary
salt and freshly ground black pepper
4 herrings, cleaned and boned
Garnish:
lemon slices

Melt the butter in the pudding basin in the microwave for 1 minute then add the onion and cook in the microwave for 3 minutes. Toss the apple in the lemon juice and add to the onion and butter together with the mustard, breadcrumbs and rosemary. Season lightly.

Divide the stuffing between the herrings and wrap them separately in greaseproof paper. Place 2 herrings in the pie dish and cook in the microwave for 3 minutes. Repeat with the second pair of herrings.

Carefully remove the greaseproof paper and place the herrings in a serving dish. Garnish with lemon slices.

Herrings in herby cream sauce

Utensils: 1-litre/2-pint round shallow ovenproof pie
dish, 600-ml/1-pint glass measuring jug
Microwave cooking time: 11 minutes 15 seconds

Serves: 4

METRIC/IMPERIAL

salt and freshly ground black
  pepper
8 herring fillets
50 g/2 oz onion, chopped
juice of ½ lemon
1 tablespoon chopped mixed
  fresh basil, thyme and
  parsley

150 ml/¼ pint fish stock
150 ml/¼ pint double cream
2 teaspoons cornflour
1 tablespoon water

Season the fish and roll up, with skin outside, from head to
tail. Secure with wooden cocktail sticks and place 4 at a
time in the pie dish. Cook in the microwave for 3 minutes.
Repeat with the other 4 fillets.

Place the onion and lemon juice in the measuring jug,
season lightly and cook in the microwave for 3 minutes. Add
the herbs, stock and cream. Heat in the microwave for 2
minutes. Blend the cornflour with the water and stir into the
sauce. Thicken in the microwave for 15 seconds, stir well and
pour a little over the fish. Serve the remaining sauce
separately.

Haddock mornay

Utensil: 1-litre/1½-pint oblong ovenproof dish
Microwave cooking time: 4–5 minutes

Serves: 4

METRIC/IMPERIAL

350 g/12 oz haddock
2 tablespoons milk
15 g/½ oz butter
2 eggs, hard-boiled and
  chopped
3 tomatoes, skinned and
  sliced
300 ml/½ pint parsley sauce
  (see page 114)

salt and freshly ground black
  pepper
50 g/2 oz cheese, grated
25 g/1 oz fresh breadcrumbs
Garnish:
stuffed olives
watercress

Place the haddock, milk and butter in the dish and cook in
the microwave for 3 minutes. Remove the fish and flake.
Return to the dish with the hard-boiled eggs, tomatoes,
parsley sauce and seasoning. Mix well and sprinkle with the
cheese and breadcrumbs. Heat in the microwave for 1–2
minutes or until the cheese has melted. Garnish with the
olives and watercress.
Note: If preferred the final cooking of the cheese and
breadcrumbs can be done under a preheated grill.

Haddock in creamy cider sauce

Utensil: 2.25-litre/4-pint deep oblong casserole
dish
Microwave cooking time: 11 minutes

Serves: 4

METRIC/IMPERIAL

450 g/1 lb haddock fillet,
  skinned
50 g/2 oz onion, chopped
50 g/2 oz button mushrooms,
  sliced

salt and freshly ground black
  pepper
300 ml/½ pint dry cider
3 teaspoons cornflour
2 teaspoons water
4 tablespoons double cream

Place the haddock in the casserole dish together with the
onion and mushrooms. Season lightly, pour over the cider

and cook in the microwave for 5 minutes, turning the fish once.

Remove the fish from the dish and keep warm. Return the sauce to the oven and cook in the microwave for a further 5 minutes, stirring twice.

Blend the cornflour with the water and add to the sauce; thicken in the microwave for 1 minute, stirring once. Stir the double cream into the sauce, taste and adjust seasoning if necessary before pouring over the fish.

Salmon quiche

Utensils: 1.75-litre/3-pint ovenproof pudding basin, 18-cm/7-inch ovenproof quiche dish, 1-litre/2-pint ovenproof soufflé dish
Microwave cooking time: 8–10 minutes

Serves: 4

METRIC/IMPERIAL

100 g/4 oz plain savoury biscuits	1 (212-g/7½-oz) can red salmon
100 g/4 oz butter	3 tablespoons milk
50 g/2 oz cheese, finely grated	grated rind of ½ lemon
Filling:	1 tablespoon chopped parsley
25 g/1 oz butter	Garnish:
50 g/2 oz onion, finely chopped	tomato slices
1 tablespoon flour	watercress sprigs

Place the biscuits in a polythene bag and crush with a rolling pin. Melt the butter in the pudding basin in the microwave for 2 minutes, then stir in the biscuits and grated cheese. Press this mixture into the base and sides of the quiche dish, chill thoroughly.

Melt the butter for the filling in the soufflé dish in the microwave for 1 minute. Add the onion and cook in the microwave for 2 minutes. Stir in the flour then carefully add the liquid from the can of salmon, milk, lemon rind and parsley. Cook in the microwave for a further 3 minutes, stirring once during cooking. Stir in the flaked salmon, mix well and fill the prepared quiche dish. Smooth the top and garnish with slices of tomato and sprigs of watercress.

Serve chilled or reheat for 2 minutes in the microwave oven, turning the dish 4 times.
Note: This quiche is best served chilled as the crunchy base provides an excellent texture variation.

Trout in white wine

Utensils: 2 cook-bags, 600-ml/1-pint ovenproof
pudding basin
Microwave cooking time: 6½ minutes

Serves: 4

METRIC/IMPERIAL

salt and freshly ground black
  pepper
4 trout, cleaned and boned
25 g/1 oz butter, melted
1 tablespoon chopped
  parsley

grated rind of 1 lemon
150 ml/¼ pint dry white wine
1 teaspoon cornflour

Season the inside of the trout and brush with melted butter.
Sprinkle the parsley and lemon rind inside the trout.

Place 2 fish in the cook-bag with the wine and secure
loosely with an elastic band. Cook in the microwave for 3
minutes. Carefully split the bag and remove the fish to a
serving dish.

Transfer the liquid to another cook-bag and cook the
remaining trout in this in the microwave for 3 minutes.
Reserve the cooking liquid and place in the pudding basin.
Blend the cornflour with a little of the liquid then stir into the
rest of the liquid and thicken in the microwave for 30
seconds. Pour over the trout before serving.

Meat, poultry and game

The microwave really comes into its own in this chapter. Joints of meat are literally cooked in minutes, for example a 1.25 kg/2¾ lb piece of beef topside can be cooked in a total of 15 minutes!

A chart giving the cooking times and defrosting times for various meats can be found on pages 88-9. Frozen meat can be successfully defrosted in the microwave in minutes, saving endless hours normally spent defrosting meat.

When making casseroles, use good quality meat as the rapid cooking of the microwave is not suitable for those cuts that require long slow cooking. Remember also that small pieces of meat cook more quickly than large pieces. If your microwave oven does not have a browning element and you want to brown chops, poultry or game for example, use a microwave browning dish (see page 14) or brown under a conventional grill.

Peppered steaks with Madeira

Utensils: 1.5-litre/2½-pint oblong shallow oven-proof dish, cook-bag
Microwave cooking time: 16 minutes

Serves: 4

METRIC/IMPERIAL

50 g/2 oz butter
1 clove garlic, crushed
2 large onions, sliced
1 green pepper, sliced
1 red pepper, sliced
5 tablespoons Madeira
salt

2 teaspoons Marmite
4 (175-g/6-oz) rump steaks
20 black peppercorns,
    crushed
Garnish:
watercress

Melt the butter in the oblong dish in the microwave for 2 minutes. Add the garlic, onions, green and red pepper. Toss well then place the dish in the cook-bag (or cover the dish with the bag split) and cook in the microwave for 5 minutes.Stir the vegetables and add 4 tablespoons of the Madeira. Season lightly with salt and replace the dish in the cook-bag. Continue to cook in the microwave for 5 minutes.

Mix the Marmite with the remaining Madeira and brush each side of the steaks with this mixture. Place them on the bed of vegetables and sprinkle the crushed peppercorns over the top. Return to the microwave and cook for 4 minutes, turning and rearranging the steaks once during cooking. (If the steaks are not cooked enough after 4 minutes for your liking, cook for a little longer.) Garnish with watercress.

Beef and walnut patties

**Utensils: 23-cm/9-inch flan dish, 600-ml/1-pint
ovenproof pudding basin
Microwave cooking time: 14 minutes**

Serves: 4

METRIC/IMPERIAL

450 g/1 lb minced beef
225 g/8 oz walnuts, finely
  chopped
2 teaspoons dried sage
1 egg
salt and freshly ground black
  pepper
Relish:
1 large onion, finely
  chopped
25 g/1 oz butter

225 g/8 oz tomatoes, peeled
  and chopped
2 teaspoons wholegrain
  mustard
2 teaspoons creamed
  horseradish
25 g/1 oz finely grated
  Cheddar cheese
Garnish:
watercress

Mix the beef with the walnuts, sage and egg. Season generously and form into 8 patties, about 7.5 cm/3 inches in diameter. Place 4 of the patties on the flan dish, as far apart as possible and cook in the microwave for 5 minutes, turning the dish around twice during cooking. Remove to a warmed serving dish and cover with foil. Cook the remaining patties and transfer to the serving dish.

For the relish, place the onion in the pudding basin with the butter and cook in the microwave for 4 minutes, stirring once during cooking. Stir in the remaining ingredients and season to taste. Serve the patties garnished with sprigs of watercress, accompanied by the onion and tomato relish.

Hungarian beef

Utensil: 2.25-litre/4-pint oblong deep ovenproof dish
Microwave cooking time: 21 minutes

Serves: 4

METRIC/IMPERIAL

25 g/1 oz butter
1 large onion, sliced
2 tablespoons flour
1 (134-g/4¾-oz) jar tomato
   purée
300 ml/½ pint brown stock

1 tablespoon paprika pepper
450 g/1 lb topside, cubed
225 g/8 oz tomatoes, skinned
   and chopped
salt and freshly ground black
   pepper

Melt the butter in the casserole dish in the microwave for 1 minute. Add the onion and cook in the microwave for a further 5 minutes. Stir in the flour and gradually add the tomato purée, stock and paprika pepper. Add the meat, stir well and cook in the microwave for 15 minutes, stirring every 2 minutes.

Stir in the tomatoes, cover with foil and leave to stand for 3–5 minutes. Adjust the seasoning before serving. Serve from the dish or transfer to a heated serving dish.

Herby meatballs

Utensil: 1.5-litre/2½-pint shallow oval ovenproof
dish
Microwave cooking time: 15 minutes

Serves: 4

METRIC/IMPERIAL

450 g/1 lb minced beef
1 medium onion, grated
6 tablespoons fresh white or
  brown breadcrumbs
½ teaspoon mixed dried
  herbs
salt and freshly ground black
  pepper
1 egg, beaten

50 g/2 oz butter
2 tablespoons flour
150 ml/¼ pint red wine
2 tablespoons tomato purée
1 beef stock cube, crumbled
300 ml/½ pint boiling water
Garnish:
chopped spring onions

Mix together the beef, onion, breadcrumbs and herbs. Season lightly and bind with the beaten egg. Shape into 16 meatballs, each about the size of a walnut.

Place the butter in the oval dish and melt in the microwave for 2 minutes. Toss the meatballs in the butter and return to the microwave for 5 minutes, turning the meatballs once during cooking. Add the flour to absorb the butter and gradually stir in the remaining ingredients. Cook in the microwave for 8 minutes, turning the meatballs 3 times during cooking. Garnish with the chopped spring onions before serving.

Chilli con carne

Utensil: 2.25-litre/4-pint oblong casserole dish
Microwave cooking time: 33 minutes

Serves: 4

METRIC/IMPERIAL

1 onion, finely chopped
1 small green pepper, finely
  chopped
2 carrots, diced
1 tablespoon oil
350 g/12 oz minced beef
150 ml/¼ pint tomato juice
150 ml/¼ pint beef stock
1 (227-g/8-oz) can tomatoes

½–1 tablespoon chilli
  powder, according to taste
salt and freshly ground black
  pepper
1 (280-g/10-oz) can kidney
  beans, drained
Garnish:
2 tablespoons chopped
  parsley

Place the onion, pepper, carrots and oil in the casserole dish and cook in the microwave for 5 minutes, stirring once. Add

the meat and continue to cook in the microwave for 4
minutes. Add all the remaining ingredients, except for the
kidney beans, cover and continue to cook for 22 minutes,
stirring twice during cooking. Stir in the kidney beans and
reheat for 2 minutes. Garnish with chopped parsley

Meatloaf with pepper sauce

**Utensils: 2.25-litre/4-pint ovenproof mixing bowl,
1-litre/1½-pint oblong ovenproof pie dish, 600-
ml/1-pint glass measuring jug
Microwave cooking time: 19 minutes**

Serves: 4

METRIC/IMPERIAL

1 tablespoon oil	Sauce:
1 large onion, chopped	25 g/1 oz butter
225 g/8 oz minced beef	100 g/4 oz green pepper,
225 g/8 oz minced pork	chopped
6 tablespoons fresh brown	1 tablespoon flour
breadcrumbs	300 ml/½ pint boiling water
1 clove garlic, crushed	1 beef stock cube
1 tablespoon tomato purée	1 tablespoon tomato purée
salt and freshly ground black	50 g/2 oz button mushrooms,
pepper	sliced
1 egg, beaten	Garnish:
	tomato wedges
	watercress

Place the oil in the mixing bowl and heat in the microwave
for 2 minutes. Add the onion and cook for 3 minutes,
stirring once. Stir in the meats, breadcrumbs, garlic and
tomato purée; season with salt and black pepper then bind
with the beaten egg. Mix well and press into the pie dish.
Cook in the microwave for 5 minutes, turning the dish twice
during cooking. Wrap completely in foil, placing the shiny
side of the foil inwards, leave to rest for 15 minutes. Remove
the foil and return to the microwave for a further 3 minutes
then wrap in foil, as before, and rest for 5 minutes.

Place the butter for the sauce in the measuring jug, and
melt in the microwave for 1 minute. Add the green pepper
and stir well; return to the microwave for 3 minutes. Stir in
the flour and carefully add the water and crumbled stock
cube, tomato purée and mushrooms. Cook in the microwave
for 2 minutes, stirring once. Taste and season the sauce. Turn
out the meatloaf and serve with some of the sauce poured
over. Garnish with tomato wedges and watercress. Serve the
remaining sauce in a jug or sauceboat.

Steak and kidney pie

Utensil: 1.5-litre/2½-pint oval ovenproof pie dish
Microwave cooking time: 40 minutes plus
conventional oven time 20–30 minutes

Serves: 4

METRIC/IMPERIAL

1 onion, thinly sliced
25 g/1 oz butter
1 tablespoon oil
450 g/1 lb chuck steak,
  cubed
100 g/4 oz ox kidney, sliced
seasoned flour
150 ml/¼ pint red wine
300 ml/½ pint beef stock
1 tablespoon Worcestershire
  sauce

1 bay leaf
mace
salt and freshly ground black
  pepper
100 g/4 oz button
  mushrooms
1 (198-g/7-oz) packet frozen
  puff pastry
1 egg, beaten

Place the onion, butter and oil in the pie dish and cook in the microwave for 4 minutes, stirring once during cooking. Toss the meat and kidney in seasoned flour and add to the onions. Cook in the microwave for 3 minutes. Add all the remaining ingredients except the mushrooms. Cover and cook in the microwave for 20 minutes, stirring frequently. Stand for 5 minutes. Cook in the microwave for a further 13 minutes. Stir in the mushrooms. Allow the meat to cool in the dish before covering with pastry.

To finish the pie, roll out the pastry to an oval shape on a lightly floured board. Cut off a thin border of pastry from the edge and line the rim of the pie dish. Dampen the edges and cover with the pastry. Seal the edges and flute. Make a hole in the centre and brush with beaten egg. Bake in a hot conventional oven (220°C, 425°F, Gas Mark 7) for 20–30 minutes.

Beef olives

Utensil: 2.25-litre/4-pint deep oblong casserole dish
Microwave cooking time: 21 minutes

Serves: 4

METRIC/IMPERIAL

25 g/1 oz dry white
  breadcrumbs
50 g/2 oz mushrooms, finely
  chopped
½ teaspoon dried mixed
  herbs
1 tablespoon lemon juice
3 tablespoons milk
salt and freshly ground black
  pepper
450 g/1 lb topside, thinly
  sliced

25 g/1 oz butter
225 g/8 oz small onions
2 tablespoons flour
450 ml/¾ pint good brown
  stock
2 tablespoons dry sherry
100 g/4 oz small button
  mushrooms
225 g/8 oz long grain rice,
cooked (see page 132)
Garnish:
chopped parsley

Mix together the breadcrumbs, chopped mushrooms, herbs,
lemon juice and milk. Season and divide this stuffing
between the slices of topside. Roll up the meat, folding in the
sides to form neat parcels and secure with string.

Place the butter in the casserole dish and melt in the
microwave for 1 minute, then add the onions and cook for a
further 5 minutes. Stir in the flour and carefully add the
stock, sherry and mushrooms. Stir well.

Place the meat in the dish with the sauce and cook in the
microwave for 15 minutes, turning the meat over and round
every 2 minutes. Leave to stand for 3 minutes before
transferring to a serving dish.

Serve on a bed of hot rice and arrange the mushrooms and
onions from the sauce on top of the beef olives; string
removed. Garnish with a little choppped parsley before
serving.

Boeuf à la bourguignonne

Utensil: 1.5-litre/2½-pint oval ovenproof pie dish
Microwave cooking time: 41 minutes

Serves: 4

METRIC/IMPERIAL

4 rashers bacon, cut into
  strips
1 onion, chopped
450 g/1 lb chuck steak,
  cubed
300 ml/½ pint beef stock
150 ml/¼ pint red wine
1 clove garlic, crushed
bouquet garni

salt and freshly ground black
  pepper
8 button onions, peeled and
  left whole
100 g/4 oz button
  mushrooms
Garnish:
2 tablespoons chopped
  parsley

Place the bacon and onion in the pie dish and cook in the
microwave for 4 minutes, stirring every minute. Add the meat
and cook in the microwave for 2 minutes. Stir in the stock,
red wine, garlic, bouquet garni, seasoning and button onions
and cook in the microwave for 30 minutes, stirring 3 times
during cooking. Add the mushrooms and cook for a further 5
minutes. Allow to stand for 5 minutes before serving.
  Garnish with chopped parsley.

Beef with almonds

Utensils: 1.75-litre/3-pint shallow oblong
ovenproof dish. 300-ml/½-pint glass measuring
jug
Microwave cooking time: 10½ minutes

Serves: 4

METRIC/IMPERIAL

450 g/1 lb topside of beef,
  trimmed
100 g/4 oz lean bacon,
  derinded and chopped
100 g/4 oz whole blanched
  almonds
2 tablespoons olive oil

salt and freshly ground black
  pepper
3 tablespoons brandy
150 ml/¼ pint soured cream
2 tablespoons chopped
  parsley

Cut the topside into thin slices and then slice each one
diagonally into strips. Place in the dish with the bacon,
almonds and olive oil. Mix well and season to taste. Cook in

the microwave for 10 minutes, stirring 4 times during cooking. Set aside.

Warm the brandy in the measuring jug in the microwave for 30 seconds, flame and immediately pour over the beef. Stir in the soured cream and parsley. Serve immediately with buttered noodles and a crisp green salad.

Tipsy kidneys

**Utensils: 1.5-litre/2½-pint oval ovenproof pie dish,
1.5-litre/2½-pint ovenproof pudding basin
Microwave cooking time: 27–28 minutes**

Serves: 4

METRIC/IMPERIAL

1 onion, finely chopped	4 frankfurters, sliced
15 g/½ oz butter	100 g/4 oz button mushrooms
1 tablespoon oil	3 tablespoons whisky or sherry
10 lambs' kidneys, skinned, cored and halved	450 ml/¾ pint hand hot water (about 48°C/120°F)
1 tablespoon flour	225 g/8 oz long grain rice
salt and freshly ground black pepper	½ teaspoon salt
2 tablespoons tomato purée	Garnish:
300 ml/½ pint chicken stock, made with a stock cube	chopped parsley

Place the onion, butter and oil in the oval dish and cook in the microwave for 4 minutes, stirring once. Stir in the kidneys and return to the microwave for 5 minutes, stirring once during cooking. Add the flour and mix well, then add all the remaining ingredients, except the whisky or sherry, water , rice and salt. Cook in the microwave for 8 minutes. Stir in the whisky or sherry and allow to stand while cooking the rice.

Place the water, rice and salt in the pudding basin and cook in the microwave for 10–11 minutes. Stir well, arrange a border round the edge of a warmed serving dish and place the kidneys in centre. Garnish with chopped parsley.

Kidney and mushroom casserole

Utensil: 2.25-litre/4-pint ovenproof mixing bowl
Microwave cooking time: 17 minutes

Serves: 4

METRIC/IMPERIAL

225 g/8 oz pickling onions, peeled
50 g/2 oz butter
2 tablespoons flour
450 g/1 lb whole lambs' kidneys, skinned and cored
150 ml/¼ pint red wine

150 ml/¼ pint boiling chicken stock
salt and freshly ground black pepper
225 g/8 oz button mushrooms
Garnish:
2 tablespoons chopped parsley

Place the onions in the mixing bowl with the butter and cook in the microwave for 4 minutes. Stir in the flour, then add the kidneys. Cook in the microwave for 7 minutes, stirring 3 times during cooking. Add the wine, stock and seasoning and cook in the microwave for a further 4 minutes, stirring once during cooking. Add the mushrooms and cook in the microwave for 2 minutes. Sprinkle with chopped parsley and serve immediately with rice or noodles.

Mexican liver

Utensil: 2.25-litre/4-pint deep oblong ovenproof dish
Microwave cooking time: 12 minutes

Serves: 4

METRIC/IMPERIAL

2 tablespoons oil
1 onion, sliced
1 (100-g/4-oz) green pepper, sliced
1 clove garlic, crushed
225 g/8 oz lamb's liver, sliced

100 g/4 oz button mushrooms
1 (397-g/14-oz) can tomatoes
3 tablespoons water
salt and freshly ground black pepper

Heat the oil in the dish in the microwave for 2 minutes. Add the onion, green pepper and garlic and cook in the microwave for 4 minutes, stirring once during cooking. Add the liver and cook in the microwave for a further minute

before mixing in the remaining ingredients. Season and
continue to cook in the microwave for a final 5 minutes,
stirring once during cooking. Leave to stand for a few
minutes before serving.

Spicy liver

Utensil: 2.25-litre/4-pint ovenproof mixing bowl
Microwave cooking time: 10 minutes

Serves: 4

METRIC/IMPERIAL

1 large onion, chopped
2 tablespoons grated root
  ginger
¼ teaspoon ground cloves
grated rind and juice of 1
  large orange
50 g/2 oz butter
salt and freshly ground black
  pepper

100 g/4 oz lean bacon,
  chopped
675 g/1½ lb lambs' liver, cut
  into strips
3 tablespoons red wine or
  chicken stock
Garnish:
1 orange, sliced

Place the onion, ginger and cloves in the mixing bowl with
the orange rind and butter. Season and cook in the
microwave for 2 minutes. Add the bacon and liver and cook
for a further 4 minutes, stirring once during cooking. Add the
orange juice and wine or stock and cook for a further 4
minutes, stirring once during cooking.

    Serve immediately with saffron rice, garnished with halved
orange slices.

Somerset gammon steaks

Utensil: 2.25-litre/4-pint deep oblong casserole
dish
Microwave cooking time: 19 minutes

Serves: 4

METRIC/IMPERIAL

4 gammon steaks
50 g/2 oz onion, thinly sliced
300 ml/½ pint apple juice
1 heaped teaspoon cornflour

1 large eating apple
juice of ½ lemon
Garnish:
watercress sprigs

Place the gammon steaks in the casserole dish and cook in
the microwave for 6 minutes, turning the steaks over and
round once. Add the onion rings, rearrange the gammon and
return to the microwave for a further 4 minutes.

Remove the gammon from the dish and add the apple
juice to the onion. Cook in the microwave for 5 minutes.
Blend the cornflour with a little of the cooking liquid then stir
back into the dish. Continue to cook in the microwave for 2
minutes, stirring twice during cooking.

Core the apple and cut into rings, leaving the skin on to
provide colour. Dip each apple ring in lemon juice to prevent
discoloration and garnish each gammon steak with an apple
ring. Pour the sauce into a sauceboat and reheat the
gammon steaks in the casserole dish for 2 minutes.

Transfer to a serving plate, garnish with watercress and
serve with the sauce.

Hawaiian pork

Utensil: 3.5-litre/6-pint ovenproof mixing bowl
Microwave cooking time: 12 minutes

Serves: 4

METRIC/IMPERIAL

450 g/1 lb pork tenderloin
2 tablespoons salted black
  beans, soaked and drained
25 g/1 oz butter
1 fresh pineapple
salt and freshly ground black
  pepper

1 bunch spring onions,
  trimmed and chopped
150 ml/¼ pint soured cream
100 g/4 oz fresh coconut,
  grated

Cut the pork in half lengthways and cut each half diagonally into thin strips. Place in the mixing bowl with the black beans and butter and cook in the microwave for 6 minutes, stirring twice during cooking. Cut the pineapple in half lengthways, scoop out the flesh and cut it into cubes . Add these to the meat mixture, season well and cook in the microwave for 2 minutes. Stir in the spring onions and cook in the microwave for a further 4 minutes stirring once during cooking. Place the pineapple halves on a serving dish and fill with the meat mixture. Mix the soured cream with the coconut and spoon over the pineapple. Serve immediately.

Lemon pork slices

Utensils: 600-ml/1-pint glass measuring jug, 1.75 - litre/3-pint shallow oblong ovenproof flan dish
Microwave cooking time: 14 minutes

Serves: 4

METRIC/IMPERIAL

1 lemon	75 g/3 oz dark brown sugar
1 large onion, finely chopped	4 tablespoons ginger wine
1 clove garlic, crushed	salt and freshly ground black pepper
50 g/2 oz butter	450 g/1 lb pork tenderloin

Halve the lemon, remove any pips and chop finely. Put the lemon, onion, garlic and butter in the jug and cook in the microwave for 2 minutes. Stir in the sugar, ginger wine and seasoning. Cut the tenderloin lengthways into 2 long slices. Cut each slice in half across and beat out thinly between 2 sheets of greaseproof paper. Arrange in the flan dish and pour over the lemon sauce. Cook in the microwave for 12 minutes, turning the meat over and basting with the sauce 4 times during cooking. Cover the dish with foil, placing the shiny side inwards to reflect the heat back into the meat and leave to stand for 3 minutes. Serve with new potatoes and a crisp salad.
Note: This recipe also works well when veal fillet is substituted for the pork.

Somerset pork with cider cream sauce

Utensil: 2.25-litre/4-pint oval casserole dish
Microwave cooking time: 26 minutes

Serves: 4

METRIC/IMPERIAL

25 g/1 oz butter
225 g/8 oz onions, chopped
0.75 kg/1½ lb pork fillet,
* trimmed and cubed*
100 g/4 oz button
* mushrooms, sliced*
300 ml/½ pint dry cider

salt and freshly ground black
* pepper*
2 tablespoons cornflour
1 tablespoon water
2 tablespoons double cream
Garnish:
chopped parsley

Place the butter in the casserole dish and melt in the microwave for 1 minute. Add the onion and cook for a further 5 minutes. Stir in the cubed pork and cook in the microwave for 8 minutes, stirring 4 times. Add the mushrooms and cider and season lightly. Cook in the microwave for 10 minutes, stirring 4 times. Blend the cornflour with the water and stir into the casserole then return to the microwave for a further 2 minutes.

Stir the double cream into the sauce and garnish with parsley.

Note: If you prefer the meat to be browner, seal the pork under a preheated grill before cooking in the microwave. The timing will be slightly reduced if this method is chosen.

Prune and almond stuffed pork

**Utensils: 1-litre/2-pint ovenproof pudding basin,
2.25-litre/4-pint oblong ovenproof dish or
microwave browning dish
Microwave cooking time: 41 minutes**

Serves: 4–6

METRIC/IMPERIAL

225 g/8 oz prunes, stoned
 and chopped
450 ml/¾ pint boiling
 chicken stock
50 g/2 oz blanched whole
 almonds

1.5 kg/3 lb boned and
 skinned belly and hand of
 pork
225 g/8 oz streaky bacon
 rashers
2 tablespoons clear honey

Mix the prunes and chicken stock together in the pudding
basin and cook in the microwave for 20 minutes, stirring
every 5 minutes, until all the water is absorbed. Mix in the
blanched almonds.

Lay the pork flat on a clean surface, skinned side
downwards. Slit the hand end of the joint with a sharp knife
and open out flat. Spread the prune stuffing over the pork
and carefully bring the two sides of the meat together, to
enclose the stuffing and form a roll. Secure firmly with string.
Brown under a pre-heated grill, if liked. Wrap the bacon
around the pork and secure with wooden cocktail sticks.
Place the meat in the oblong dish and cook in the microwave
for 10 minutes, turning over twice. Allow to stand for 10
minutes then return to the microwave for a further 5 minutes.
Again rest for 10 minutes and finally return to the microwave
for 5 minutes.

Wrap in foil, with the shiny side inwards, and leave to
stand for 20-30 minutes before serving. Remove from the foil
and place on a serving dish.

Place the honey and 1 tablespoon of the pork drippings in
the pudding basin and heat in the microwave for 1 minute.
Brush the pork with this glaze before serving.
Note: If using the microwave browning dish, there is no need
to brown the meat under the grill. Preheat the browning dish
in the microwave with 1 tablespoon oil for 4 minutes before
putting the meat in the dish (see page 14). Seal the meat on
all sides and then continue to cook as above.

Pork casserole with apple

Utensil: 2.25-litre/4-pint deep casserole dish
Microwave cooking time: 20 minutes

Serves: 4
METRIC/IMPERIAL

25 g/1 oz butter
1 large onion, quartered
1 tablespoon flour
0.75 kg/1½ lb lean pork, cut in bite-size pieces
few sprigs mixed fresh herbs, tied in a bundle

175 ml/6 fl oz dry white wine
salt and freshly ground black pepper
1 large green-skinned eating apple, cored and sliced
juice of ½ lemon
50 g/2 oz mushrooms, sliced

Cook the butter and onion in the casserole dish in the microwave for 8 minutes. Stir in the flour, add the meat and herbs and carefully stir in the wine. Season lightly and cook in the microwave for 7 minutes, stirring 3 times.

Dip the apple slices in the lemon juice to prevent discoloration and add to the casserole together with the mushrooms. Cook in the microwave for 5 minutes, stirring once during cooking. Remove the herbs from the casserole before serving.

Stuffed pork rolls

Utensils: 2.25-litre/4-pint ovenproof mixing bowl,
300-ml/½-pint ovenproof pudding basin
Microwave cooking time: 7½ minutes

Serves: 4

METRIC/IMPERIAL

1 large onion, chopped
225 g/8 oz minced pork
salt and freshly ground black pepper
1 tablespoon tomato purée
1 (156-g/5½-oz) can pâté de campagne

2 teaspoons dried sage
2 tablespoons ginger wine
4 crusty bread rolls
Topping:
25 g/1 oz roasted sesame seeds
50 g/2 oz butter

Place the onion in the mixing bowl with the minced pork and season generously. Mix well and cook in the microwave for 4 minutes, stirring once during cooking. Add the tomato purée, pâté, sage and ginger wine and mix well. Cook in the microwave for a further 2 minutes, stirring once during cooking.

Meanwhile, halve the rolls and scoop out all the bread to leave an empty, crusty shell. Reduce the middle to fine breadcrumbs and stir into the mince mixture. Place the bottom halves of the rolls on a serving dish and pile the filling on them. Top each with a remaining half.

Place the butter in the pudding basin with the sesame seeds and heat in the microwave for 1½ minutes. Pour over the rolls and serve immediately.

Ham and spinach rolls

Utensil: 1.75-litre/3-pint shallow oblong ovenproof flan dish
Microwave cooking time: 11 minutes

Serves: 4

METRIC/IMPERIAL

1 (225-g/8-oz) packet frozen spinach, defrosted and thoroughly drained
100 g/4 oz cream cheese
salt and freshly ground black pepper

8 slices cooked ham
tomato sauce (see page 111)
100 g/4 oz mushrooms, sliced

Beat the spinach into the cream cheese and season generously. Spread thickly over the ham slices then roll up and arrange side by side in the flan dish. Make the tomato sauce, adding the mushrooms after 2½ minutes of the cooking time. Pour the sauce over the ham rolls and cook in the microwave for 4 minutes, turning the dish once during cooking. Serve immediately with a crisp green salad.

Lamb with walnut and orange stuffing

**Utensils: 2.25-litre/4-pint ovenproof mixing bowl,
600-ml/1-pint ovenproof pudding basin, 3.5-litre/6-
pint oval ovenproof dish
Microwave cooking time: 29 minutes**

Serves: 6

METRIC/IMPERIAL

1 small onion, chopped	2 teaspoons dried rosemary
50 g/2 oz butter	1 cooking apple, peeled,
100 g/4 oz walnuts, chopped	cored and sliced
225 g/8 oz fresh	1 (1.5-kg/3½-lb) shoulder of
breadcrumbs	lamb, boned
grated rind and juice of 2	300 ml/½ pint boiling
oranges	chicken stock
salt and freshly ground black	
pepper	

Place the onion in the mixing bowl with half the butter and
cook in the microwave for 2 minutes. Stir in the walnuts,
breadcrumbs, rind and juice of the oranges, the seasoning
and rosemary. Place the apple in the pudding basin with the
remaining butter and cook in the microwave for 2 minutes.
Add the apple to the stuffing mixture and mix well. Fill the
lamb with the stuffing and secure the opening with wooden
cocktail sticks. Place the stuffed lamb in the oval dish and
cook in the microwave for 16 minutes, turning the joint over
twice during cooking and allowing the meat to rest for 5
minutes halfway through the cooking time. To rest the meat,
wrap it tightly in foil with the shiny side inwards. Remove the
foil before cooking the meat for the second time. At the end
of the cooking time, take the meat from the dish, wrap it
tightly in a double layer of foil, shiny sides inwards, and
leave to rest for a further 10 minutes. Return the joint to the
dish and cook in the microwave for 8 minutes more, turning
the meat twice during cooking and allowing it to rest for 10
minutes half way through the cooking time as before.

Place the joint on a serving dish. Mix the chicken stock
with the meat juices in the dish and heat in the microwave
for 1 minute. Pour the gravy over the lamb to serve.

Veal with ham and mushroom sauce

Utensils: 2.25-litre/4-pint ovenproof mixing bowl,
1.75-litre/3-pint oblong ovenproof flan dish
Microwave cooking time: 10 minutes

Serves: 4

METRIC/IMPERIAL

225 g/8 oz cooked ham,
  finely chopped
225 g/8 oz mushrooms, finely
  chopped
75 g/3 oz butter
Salt and freshly ground
  black pepper

4 thin slices veal fillet,
  trimmed
2 tablespoons yogurt
Garnish:
watercress

Place the ham, mushrooms and two thirds of the butter in the
mixing bowl. Season and cook in the microwave for 3
minutes, stirring once during cooking. Arrange the veal slices
in the flan dish and dot with the remaining butter. Cook in
the microwave for 5 minutes, turning the meat and basting it
with the melted butter 4 times during cooking. Re-heat the
ham mixture in the microwave for 2 minutes. Arrange the
veal on a warmed serving dish. Top with the ham mixture
and spoon the yogurt over. Garnish with sprigs of watercress
and serve immediately.

Sweet 'n' sour lamb

Utensil: 1.5-litre/2½-pint oval ovenproof pie dish
Microwave cooking time: 27 minutes

Serves: 4

METRIC/IMPERIAL

1 onion, finely chopped
2 sticks celery, finely sliced
1 tablespoon oil
0.75 kg/1½ lb lean shoulder
  of lamb, cubed
seasoned flour
1 (396-g/14-oz) can tomatoes
2 tablespoons tomato purée

2 tablespoons wine vinegar
1 tablespoon brown sugar
300 ml/½ pint stock
1 tablespoon redcurrant jelly
1 teaspoon dried basil
salt and freshly ground black
  pepper

Place the onion, celery and oil in the pie dish and cook in
the microwave for 5 minutes, stirring twice during cooking.
Toss the meat in seasoned flour and add to the vegetables.
Cook in the microwave for 2 minutes. Add the remaining
ingredients, cover and continue to cook in the microwave for
20 minutes, stirring twice during cooking. Allow to stand for
10 minutes before serving.

Quick lamb chops

**Utensils: 1.5-litre/2½-pint shallow oblong
casserole dish, 23-cm/9-inch round ovenproof
dinner plate, kitchen paper
Microwave cooking time: 11 minutes**

Serves: 3

METRIC/IMPERIAL
75 g/3 oz softened butter
grated rind of 1 lemon
1 teaspoon lemon juice
6 lamb chops
garlic salt
freshly ground black pepper
3 firm tomatoes
Garnish:
watercress

Beat the softened butter with the lemon rind and juice. Place
the chops in the oblong dish and dot each with the lemon
butter. Reserve a little butter for the tomatoes. Season with a
little garlic salt and freshly ground black pepper then cook
in the microwave for 10 minutes, turning the chops over and
rearranging them 3 times during cooking.

Place the tomatoes on the dinner plate and surround them
by kitchen paper (this helps to support the tomatoes and
prevent them from collapsing). Cut a cross in the top of each
tomato and dot with the remaining lemon butter. Cook in
the microwave for 1 minute, turning the plate once during
cooking. Arrange the chops on a serving dish together with
the tomatoes and garnish with watercress. If liked, serve with
jacket potatoes cooked in the microwave oven (see pages
98-9).

Lamb in onion and caraway sauce

Utensil: 2.25-litre/4-pint deep round ovenproof dish
Microwave cooking time: 20 minutes

Serves: 4

METRIC/IMPERIAL

50 g/2 oz butter
100 g/4 oz onion, chopped
0.75 kg/1½ lb lean lamb
  (e.g. boned fillet from leg)
2 tablespoons flour

1 teaspoon tarragon vinegar
1 tablespoon caraway seeds
300 ml/½ pint boiling stock
salt and freshly ground black
  pepper

Melt the butter in the dish in the microwave for 1 minute.
Add the onion and cook in the microwave for 2 minutes. Cut
the lamb into cubes, add to the onion and continue to cook
in the microwave for 7 minutes, stirring twice.

Stir in the flour, tarragon vinegar and caraway seeds then
carefully add the stock. Season lightly and thicken in the
microwave for 10 minutes, stirring 4 times. Taste and adjust
seasoning before serving with boiled rice.

Chicken and water chestnut pilaf

Utensils: 2.25-litre/4-pint oblong casserole dish,
600-ml/1-pint glass measuring jug
Microwave cooking time: 26 minutes

Serves: 4

METRIC/IMPERIAL

1 onion, finely chopped
15 g/½ oz butter
1 tablespoon oil
4 chicken breasts
300 ml/½ pint apple juice
¼ teaspoon turmeric
salt and freshly ground black
  pepper
1 (227-g/8-oz) can water
  chestnuts, drained and
  sliced

10 stuffed olives, halved
1 tablespoon cornflour
Pilaf rice:
300 ml/½ pint hand hot
  water (about 48°C/120°F)
100 g/4 oz long grain rice
¼ teaspoon turmeric
Garnish:
chopped parsley

Place the onion, butter and oil in the casserole and cook in the microwave for 5 minutes, stirring twice. Add the chicken to the dish and cook for 4 minutes, turning over after 2 minutes.

Stir in the apple juice, turmeric and seasoning, and cook in the microwave for 5 minutes. Add the water chestnuts and olives, continue to cook for a further 2 minutes. Blend the cornflour with a little water and stir into the chicken mixture. Cover and allow to stand whilst cooking the rice.

For the pilaf rice, place all the ingredients in the measuring jug and cook in the microwave for 10 minutes. Stir well and serve with the chicken piled on top. Garnish with chopped parsley.

Chicken with vegetables in wine

Utensils: 600-ml/1-pint oval ovenproof pie dish
1.75-litre/3-pint oblong ovenproof dish, 1.5-litre/2½-pint shallow oblong ovenproof dish
Microwave cooking time: 31 minutes

Serves: 4

METRIC/IMPERIAL

1 (1.5-kg/3¼-lb) chicken
25 g/1 oz butter
225 g/8 oz small onions, peeled
225 g/8 oz carrots, thickly sliced
100 g/4 oz streaky bacon, chopped
1 green pepper, deseeded and chopped

2 sticks celery, sliced
100 g/4 oz small button mushrooms
1 bay leaf
salt and freshly ground black pepper
2 tablespoons flour
300 ml/½ pint medium dry white wine
300 ml/½ pint chicken stock

Tie the legs of the chicken together firmly to hold them as closely to the body of the bird as possible. Place the chicken on the upturned pie dish in the larger oblong dish. Cook in the microwave for 5 minutes, turning the dish round and the bird over at the end of the cooking time. Continue to cook in the microwave for a further 10 minutes, again turning the bird over 4 times and turning the dish round twice during the cooking time.

Wrap the chicken in a double thickness of foil with the shiny side inwards and allow to stand for 20-30 minutes before serving.

Melt the butter in the shallow dish in the microwave for 1

minute then add the onions, carrots, bacon, pepper and celery. Cook in the microwave for a further 5 minutes before adding the mushrooms and bay leaf. Season lightly and stir in the flour. Add the wine and stock and thicken in the microwave for 10 minutes, stirring twice.

Brown the chicken under a conventional grill, if liked, and then place in a serving dish. Arrange the vegetables in wine round the chicken.

Chicken tandoori

**Utensil: 1-litre/2-pint shallow round ovenproof dish
Microwave cooking time: 20 minutes:**

Serves: 4

METRIC/IMPERIAL

4 chicken breasts	½ teaspoon turmeric
150 ml/¼ pint plain yogurt	½ teaspoon garlic salt
grated rind of ½ lemon	salt and freshly ground black
1 tablespoon ground ginger	pepper

Slash the chicken at intervals, taking care only to penetrate halfway through the flesh. Mix the remaining ingredients together and spread over the chicken, pressing well in between the cuts. Cover with cling film and leave overnight.

Place in the shallow dish, cover with any remaining yogurt mixture and cook in the microwave for 5 minutes, turn the dish a quarter turn and continue to cook for a further 5 minutes. Alter the position of the chicken pieces and return to the microwave for 10 minutes, giving the dish a quarter turn after 5 minutes.

Chicken and artichoke casserole

Utensil: 2.25-litre/4-pint oblong casserole dish
Microwave cooking time: 25 minutes

Serves : 4

METRIC/IMPERIAL

4 chicken breasts	150 ml/¼ pint chicken stock
25 g/1 oz flour	grated rind of ½ lemon
½ teaspoon paprika pepper	salt and freshly ground black
25 g/1 oz butter	pepper
1 small onion, finely	1 tablespoon dried tarragon
chopped	1 (400-g/14-oz) can
150 ml/¼ pint white wine	artichoke hearts
	150 ml/¼ pint soured cream

Skin the chicken and toss in the mixed flour and paprika
pepper. Place the butter in the casserole and melt in the
microwave for 1 minute. Add the floured chicken, cook in the
microwave for 2 minutes, turn over and continue to cook for
3 minutes. Remove the chicken and stir in the onion. Return
to the microwave for 5 minutes, stirring frequently. Add any
remaining flour, the wine, stock, lemon rind, seasoning and
tarragon. Return to the microwave for 4 minutes then replace
the chicken in the casserole. Cover and cook in the
microwave for 8 minutes. Stir in the drained artichokes and
continue to cook in the microwave for 2 minutes. Lightly stir
in the soured cream before serving.

Chicken with onion and olive sauce

Utensil: 1.75-litre/3-pint oblong ovenproof dish
Microwave cooking time: 18 minutes

Serves: 4

METRIC/IMPERIAL

1 large onion, chopped	300 ml/½ pint boiling
50 g/2 oz butter	chicken stock
4 boned chicken breasts,	salt and freshly ground black
about 175 g/6 oz each	pepper
100 g/4 oz stuffed green	2 teaspoons cornflour
olives, halved	3 tablespoons port

Place the onion in the dish, add the butter and cook in the microwave for 2 minutes. Add the chicken, arranging the pieces as far apart as possible and sprinkle with the olives. Cook in the microwave for 10 minutes, turning the dish around and the pieces of chicken over 4 times during cooking.

Stir in the stock and season to taste. Cook in the microwave for 2 minutes. Blend the cornflour with the port and stir into the sauce. Cook in the microwave for 4 minutes, stirring once during cooking. Serve with rice and a crunchy salad.

Rolled galantine of chicken

Utensils: 2.25-litre/4-pint oblong ovenproof dish, 1-litre/2-pint ovenproof soufflé dish, large oval shallow ovenproof meat dish (about 33 × 23 cm/13 × 9 inches)
Microwave cooking time: To defrost the chicken: 20 minutes. For the rolled galantine: 20 minutes

Serves: 4

METRIC/IMPERIAL

1 frozen (1.5-kg/3½-lb) chicken, defrosted (see method) and boned

100 g/4 oz onion, finely chopped

100 g/4 oz cooked ham, chopped

100 g/4 oz cooked tongue, chopped

225 g/8 oz sausagemeat

1 tablespoon chopped fresh mixed herbs

2 tablespoons sherry

2 tablespoons chopped black olives

1 tablespoon chopped stuffed olives

salt and freshly ground black pepper

Garnish:
tomato wedges
watercress sprigs

Defrosting the chicken

To defrost the chicken, place the bird, breastside uppermost, in the oblong dish, having first opened the bag and removed any metal ties from the bird. Defrost in the microwave for 2 minutes and turn the chicken over, breastside down. Return to the microwave for 2 minutes more. Turn the bird over and rest for 5 minutes. Repeat this process 4 times more. Wrap the chicken in a double thickness of foil, placing the shiny side inwards to reflect the heat back into the bird. Leave to stand for 20 minutes then remove the giblets. Rinse the cavity with boiling water to ensure it is thoroughly defrosted.

Place the onion in the soufflé dish and cook in the microwave for 5 minutes. Add the ham, tongue and sausagemeat. Mix well then stir in the herbs, sherry and chopped olives; season lightly.

Bone the chicken and place, skin side down, on a board. Have ready a large needle threaded with double cotton—preferably in a colour easy to distinguish for removal. Spread the stuffing out over the chicken, splitting the legs down one side. Roll the chicken up from head to tail, tucking in any protruding flesh, to form a long thin sausage. Sew up firmly with the double cotton and place on the large oval meat dish. Cook in the microwave for 15 minutes, turning the dish round 3 times and turning the chicken over every 5 minutes. Remove any excess drippings with a baster during the cooking time. Remove the string from the chicken and wrap in foil, shiny side inwards, then allow to stand for 15 minutes before serving. Garnish with wedges of tomato and watercress before serving. This is also excellent served cold.

Note: The chicken was rolled from head to tail and not reshaped in the traditional way to produce a uniform shape which would cook particularly successfully in the microwave oven.

Oriental oranges

Utensil: 1-litre/2-pint ovenproof pudding basin
Microwave cooking time: 11 minutes

Serves: 4

METRIC/IMPERIAL

450 g/1 lb uncooked turkey, chicken or duck meat, shredded	50 g/2 oz mushrooms, sliced
	2 tablespoons soy sauce
	1 tablespoon cornflour
50 g/2 oz butter	3 tablespoons sherry
4 large oranges	salt and freshly ground black pepper
1 (227-g/8 oz-can) water chestnuts, sliced	

Mix the turkey with the butter in the pudding basin and cook for 6 minutes in the microwave, stirring 3 times during cooking.

Cut small caps off the oranges and scoop out all the centres. Squeeze as much juice as possible out of the pulp and strain. Add the water chestnuts, mushrooms and soy sauce to the turkey together with the orange juice. Blend the cornflour with the sherry and stir into the mixture. Season to taste and cook in the microwave for 5 minutes, stirring 3 times during cooking.

Arrange the oranges on a serving dish and fill with the turkey mixture. Top with the caps and serve immediately.

Pâté-stuffed chicken

**Utensils: 1.15-litre/2-pint ovenproof pudding basin,
1.75-litre/3-pint oblong ovenproof dish
Microwave cooking time: 21 minutes**

Serves: 4–6

METRIC/IMPERIAL

1 small onion, finely chopped	50 g/2 oz fresh breadcrumbs
25 g/1 oz butter	225 g/8 oz pâté de campagne
salt and freshly ground black pepper	1 (1.5-kg/3¼-lb) chicken
2 tablespoons chopped mixed fresh herbs, e.g. parsley, thyme, sage, rosemary, chives	1 tablespoon flour
	300 ml/½ pint boiling chicken stock
	a little gravy browning

Place the onion in the basin with the butter and cook in the microwave for 4 minutes. Season generously and add the herbs and breadcrumbs. Stir in the pâté and spoon the stuffing mixture into the body cavity of the chicken.

Cook in the microwave according to the instructions on page 83. Remove from the dish and wrap in foil with the shiny side inwards. Drain any excess fat from the cooking dish and stir in the flour. Add the stock and cook in the microwave for 2 minutes. Stir in gravy browning to taste and pour a little over the chicken before serving.

Pigeons in red wine

Utensil: microwave browning dish
Microwave cooking time: 28 minutes

Serves: 4

METRIC/IMPERIAL

25 g/1 oz butter
1 tablespoon oil
2 pigeons, drawn and
   trussed
4 rashers streaky bacon
1 onion, finely chopped
1 tablespoon flour
2 tablespoons redcurrant
   jelly
150 ml/¼ pint red wine
150 ml/¼ pint stock

1 tablespoon tomato purée
salt and freshly ground black
   pepper
100 g/4 oz button
   mushrooms
50 g/2 oz stuffed olives
2 tablespoons chopped
   parsley
Garnish:
watercress

Place the browning dish in the microwave without the lid, and heat in the microwave empty for 4 minutes. Add the butter and oil then place the pigeons, each wrapped in 2 rashers of bacon, in the heated dish. Cook in the microwave for 4 minutes, turning the birds frequently, so they are browned on all sides. Remove the birds and stir in the onion. Cover and cook in the microwave for 2 minutes. Stir in the flour, redcurrant jelly, wine, stock, tomato purée and seasoning, and return to the microwave for 2 minutes. Stir well and return the birds to the dish. Cover and cook in the microwave for 8 minutes, turning the dish and the birds after 4 minutes. Cook for a further 4 minutes then add the mushrooms, olives and parsley. Cook for 4 minutes. Allow to stand for a few minutes before serving. Garnish with watercress.
Note: If the birds are too high in the dish for the lid to be used, cover with cling film.

   Timing of this dish may vary according to the age of the pigeons.

Meat roasting chart

Instructions for roasting a joint

1. Calculate the cooking time required (see chart on pages 88-9).
2. Place the joint on an upturned plate in a large dish. Cook in the microwave for approximately 5 minutes at a time, allowing a 5-minute resting time between each cooking period, until the total microwave cooking time is reached.
3. Wrap in foil (with the shiny side inwards) and stand for 15–30 minutes, or the remaining resting time, until the meat is cooked through.

This is only a guide, as times will vary according to the shape and size of the meat, and also personal taste.

Instructions for defrosting and cooking a frozen joint

1. Weigh the joint to determine the time necessary to defrost it prior to cooking (see chart).
2. Place the joint on an upturned plate in a large dish and defrost in the microwave for approximately 5 minutes at a time, allowing resting periods of 5 minutes between each , until the total calculated defrosting time is reached.
3. Wrap the joint in foil (shiny side inwards) and rest for the remaining suggested resting time, or until the joint is completely thawed.
4. Proceed to cook as for a fresh joint.

Example

Taking a 1.25 kg/2¾ lb beef topside–frozen.

Total defrosting time = 16 minutes
Resting time (when defrosting) = 60 minutes
Total microwave cooking time = 15 minutes
Resting time (when cooking) = 35–40 minutes

Following the instructions, place the joint on an upturned plate in a large dish and defrost for four 4-minute periods in the microwave oven, allowing 5-minute resting intervals between each cooking period. Wrap in foil (shiny side inwards) and leave to stand for 45 minutes, or until the joint has defrosted completely.

Unwrap the joint and replace it on the plate then cook in the microwave oven for three periods of 5 minutes, allowing a 5-minute resting interval between each cooking period. Wrap in foil, (shiny side inwards) and stand for 25–30 minutes before serving.

Cut of meat	Weight of joint	Total microwave cooking time	Total resting time
Beef, topside (medium rare)	1.25 kg/2¾ lb	15 minutes	35–40 minutes
Beef, rolled rib roast (medium)	1.5 kg/3 lb	20 minutes	30–40 minutes
Lamb, unboned fillet off leg (well cooked)	1 kg/2 lb	15 minutes	35 minutes
Lamb, shoulder boned and rolled (well cooked)	1.25 kg/2½ lb	20 minutes	30–40 minutes
Pork, unboned fillet off leg	1.5 kg/3 lb	25 minutes	30–40 minutes
Chicken, whole, unboned	1.5 kg/3¼ lb	15 minutes	30 minutes
Duck, whole, unboned	2 kg/4¾ lb	20 minutes	20 minutes

| Microwave cooking time per 0.5 kg/1 lb | Additional time from frozen | | Microwave defrosting time per 0.5 kg/1 lb |
	Total microwave defrosting time	Resting time	
5 minutes	16 minutes	60 minutes	5 minutes
6-7 minutes	16 minutes	55 minutes	5 minutes
7 minutes	9 minutes	35 minutes	4-5 minutes
8 minutes	10 minutes	45-55 minutes	4 minutes
8-9 minutes	12 minutes	40-50 minutes	4-5 minutes
4½-5 minutes	12 minutes	40 minutes	3½-4 minutes
4-5 minutes	16 minutes	45 minutes	3½-4 minutes

Vegetable dishes

Vegetables are very successfully cooked in the microwave oven, and are often superior in flavour, colour and texture to those cooked by conventional methods. As there is little or no water needed when using a cook-bag, the nutrients are retained (see chart on pages 107-9). Care should be taken when using cook-bags as the steam builds up inside. It is advisable to secure the end of the bag loosely with an elastic band, so that excess steam can escape. Handle the bags carefully, preferably with a tea-towel, to prevent any burning from the steam. Left in the cook-bag the vegetables will remain hot for some time. This is particularly useful when preparing a meal as there is then no need for the vegetables to be reheated.

Vegetables may also be cooked in a suitable dish, preferably covered. The cooking time is then longer as more liquid is required.

The amount of time saved by cooking vegetables in the microwave varies according to the vegetable. Those with a high water content cook more quickly than those with a low water content. Cooking times are also affected by age and size, older vegetables taking longer to cook.

Tuna-stuffed peppers

Utensils: 600-ml/1-pint glass measuring jug, 1-litre/2-pint ovenproof pudding basin, 1-litre/2-pint round shallow ovenproof dish
Microwave cooking time: 24 minutes

Serves: 4

METRIC/IMPERIAL

100 g/4 oz long grain rice
300 ml/½ pint hand hot
   water (about 48°C/120°F)
½ teaspoon salt
4 green or red peppers
   (about 75 g/3 oz each)
50 g/2 oz onion, chopped
25 g/1 oz butter

1 (198-g/7-oz) can tuna,
   drained
1 tablespoon lemon juice
100 g/4 oz cucumber, peeled
   and chopped
50 g/2 oz mature Cheddar
   cheese, finely grated
salt and freshly ground black
   pepper

n the measuring jug, mix the rice with the water and salt
nd cook in the microwave for 10 minutes. Cut the tops off
he peppers and remove the seeds and pith from the insides.
n the pudding basin, mix the onion and butter and cook in
he microwave for 2 minutes. Add the fish, lemon juice,
:ucumber and cheese. Stir in the cooked rice and season to
aste. Pile this mixture into the peppers and place them in
he round shallow dish. Pour 150 ml/¼ pint hand hot water
n the dish and cook in the microwave for 12 minutes. Serve
vith a tomato sauce (see page 111), if liked.

Savoury-stuffed tomatoes

Utensils: 1-litre/2-pint ovenproof pudding basin, 1-litre/2-pint round shallow ovenproof dish, kitchen paper
Microwave cooking time: 3 minutes

Serves: 4

METRIC/IMPERIAL

4 tomatoes, about 75 g/3 oz
  each
100 g/4 oz cooked ham,
  chopped
50 g/2 oz onion, grated
25 g/1 oz fresh fine
  breadcrumbs

50 g/2 oz mushrooms,
  chopped
1 small packet salted crisps,
  crushed
1 tablespoon grated
  Parmesan cheese
Garnish:
parsley sprigs

Cut the tops off the tomatoes and scoop out the centre flesh.
Mix this with the ham, onion, breadcrumbs and mushrooms in
the pudding basin and cook in the microwave for 2 minutes.
Fill the tomatoes with this mixture and place them in the
shallow dish. Prop the tomatoes up if necessary with kitchen
paper and heat in the microwave for 1 minute.

Mix together the crushed crisps and Parmesan cheese and
sprinkle on top of each tomato. Garnish each with a parsley
sprig and serve hot.

Stuffed cabbage leaves

Utensils: 3.5-litre/6-pint ovenproof mixing bowl,
2.25-litre/4-pint ovenproof mixing bowl, cook-bag,
600-ml/1-pint glass measuring jug
Microwave cooking time: 14 minutes

Serves: 4

METRIC/IMPERIAL

8 large cabbage leaves
1.75 litres/3 pints hot water
Stuffing:
225 g/8 oz garlic sausage, chopped
50 g/2 oz button mushrooms, chopped
2 tablespoons grated onion
4 tablespoons fresh brown breadcrumbs
1 egg, beaten

salt and freshly ground black pepper
Sauce:
1 (396-g/14-oz) can tomatoes
1 bay leaf
½ teaspoon dried mixed herbs
1 beef stock cube, crumbled
2 tablespoons tomato purée
2 teaspoons cornflour

Place the cabbage leaves in the larger mixing bowl with the hot water and blanch in the microwave for 3 minutes until they are just cooked. Drain well. In the smaller mixing bowl mix together the ingredients for the stuffing and season lightly. Cook in the microwave for 3 minutes, stirring once.

Divide the stuffing between the cabbage leaves and carefully roll up, folding in the sides of the leaves to form small parcels. Carefully place them in the cook-bag, loosely seal with an elastic band and heat in the microwave for 1 minute, immediately before serving.

Place all the ingredients for the sauce , except the cornflour, in the measuring jug and cook in the microwave for 5 minutes. Strain off the liquid and reserve. Return the sauce to the jug. Blend the cornflour with a little of the reserved liquid and stir into the sauce. In the microwave thicken the sauce for 2 minutes, stirring once, and serve poured over the cabbage leaves.

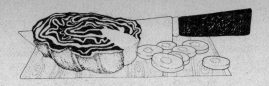

Sweet and sour red cabbage

Utensil: 2.25-litre/4-pint ovenproof mixing bowl
Microwave cooking time: 15 minutes

Serves: 4

METRIC/IMPERIAL

175 g/6 oz onion, finely
  chopped
75 g/3 oz carrot, chopped
75 g/3 oz green pepper,
  chopped
100 g/4 oz streaky bacon,
  chopped
rind and juice of 1 orange
2 tablespoons wine vinegar
1 tablespoon soy sauce

3 tablespoons dry sherry
1 heaped tablespoon brown
  sugar
2 tablespoons tomato
  ketchup
450 g/1 lb red cabbage,
  coarsely shredded
2 teaspoons cornflour
1 tablespoon water

In the bowl, mix together the onion, carrot, green pepper
and bacon and cook in the microwave for 2 minutes. Add the
orange rind and juice, wine vinegar, soy sauce, sherry,
sugar, tomato ketchup and stir well. Toss the cabbage in the
sauce and cook in the microwave for 8 minutes, stirring every
2 minutes.

Blend the cornflour with the water and stir into the
cabbage mixture. Thicken in the microwave for a further 4
minutes, stirring twice during cooking.

Ratatouille

Utensils: 600-ml/1-pint ovenproof pudding basin,
cook-bag
Microwave cooking time: 9 minutes

Serves: 4

METRIC/IMPERIAL

1 medium onion, sliced
1 clove garlic, crushed
1 green pepper, deseeded
and finely chopped
25 g/1 oz butter
175 g/6 oz courgettes, cut
into chunks

1 aubergine, cut into chunks
salt and freshly ground black
pepper
450 g/1 lb tomatoes, skinned
and chopped
2 tablespoons chopped
parsley

Place the onion, garlic and green pepper in the pudding
basin with the butter and cook in the microwave for 3
minutes. Transfer the onion mixture to the cook-bag and add
the courgettes, aubergine and seasoning. Secure loosely with
an elastic band and cook in the microwave for 4 minutes.
Add the tomatoes and cook in the microwave for a further 2
minutes. Turn into a serving dish and sprinkle with chopped
parsley.

Stuffed aubergines

Utensils: 1-litre/¾-pint glass measuring jug, cook-
bag, 1.75-litre/3-pint oblong ovenproof flan dish
Microwave cooking time: 10 minutes

Serves: 4

METRIC/IMPERIAL

1 large onion, chopped
1 clove garlic, crushed
25 g/1 oz butter
4 medium aubergines
25 g/1 oz fresh breadcrumbs
1 (215-g/7½-oz) can
pilchards in tomato sauce

salt and freshly ground black
pepper
100 g/4 oz Cheddar cheese,
grated
grated rind of 1 lemon

Place the onion, garlic and butter in the jug and cook in the
microwave for 2 minutes. Cut the aubergines in half
lengthways and scoop out the flesh. Chop the aubergine flesh
and stir it into the onion mixture. Add the breadcrumbs,

pilchards, seasoning, cheese and lemon rind and mix together. Place half the aubergine shells in a cook-bag and cook in the microwave for 2 minutes. Leave them to rest for 3 minutes before removing them from the bag. Repeat with the remaining aubergines. Fill the skins with the pilchard mixture and place them in the oblong dish. Cook, 4 at a time, in the microwave for 2 minutes.

Potato and frankfurter cream

Utensils: cook-bag, 3.5-litre/6-pint ovenproof mixing bowl
Microwave cooking time: 11 minutes

Serves: 4

METRIC/IMPERIAL

1 kg/2 lb new potatoes, washed
175 g/6 oz cooking apples, peeled, cored and cubed
100 g/4 oz streaky bacon, derinded and finely chopped
225 g/8 oz frankfurters, sliced
50 g/2 oz butter
salt and freshly ground black pepper
225 g/8 oz full fat soft cheese, cubed

Place the potatoes in the cook bag, add 4 tablespoons hot water and cook in the microwave for 7 minutes. Leave to stand in the bag for 5 minutes. Put the apple, bacon, frankfurters and butter in the mixing bowl and cook in the microwave for 2 minutes. Add the potatoes, season well and cook in the microwave for a further 2 minutes. Stir in the cheese cubes and serve immediately.

Stuffed onions

**Utensils: 1-litre/2-pint ovenproof pudding basin,
cook-bag, 23-cm/9-inch flan dish.
Microwave cooking time: 28 minutes**

Serves: 4

METRIC/IMPERIAL

50 g/2 oz easy-cook rice
pinch of salt
150 ml/¼ pint boiling water
4 Spanish onions, peeled
225 g/8 oz strong garlic
   sausage, skinned and
   finely chopped

1 teaspoon wholegrain
   mustard
50 g/2 oz Cheddar cheese,
   finely grated
salt and freshly ground black
   pepper
2 tablespoons chopped
   parsley

Place the rice, salt and water in the pudding basin and cook
for 8 minutes, stirring once during cooking. Place two of the
whole onions in a cook-bag and secure the end loosely with
an elastic band. Cook in the microwave for 6 minutes.
Repeat with the remaining onions and leave until cool
enough to handle. Carefully remove the centre of the onions
and chop finely. Mix into the rice together with the garlic
sausage, mustard and cheese. Season to taste and stir in the
parsley. Press the filling into the onion shells, piling it up
slightly on top. Place the onions on the flan dish and cook in
the microwave for 8 minutes, turning the dish twice during
cooking.

Beetroot and bacon bake

Utensils: **2.25-litre/4-pint ovenproof mixing bowl,
1-litre/2-pint ovenproof pudding basin**
Microwave cooking time: 12 minutes

Serves: 4–6

METRIC/IMPERIAL

1 small crusty white loaf
1 large onion, chopped
225 g/8 oz lean bacon,
   derinded and chopped
675 g/1½ lb cooked
   beetroot, cubed
300 ml/½ pint soured cream
50 g/1 2 oz butter

½ teaspoon grated nutmeg
salt and freshly ground black
   pepper
300 ml/½ pint milk
225 g/8 oz sage Derby
   cheese, cubed
1 tablespoon chopped chives

Halve the loaf horizontally across the middle and scoop out
as much of the bread as possible to leave a thin, crusty shell.
Reduce the scooped-out bread to fine crumbs.

Mix the onion and bacon in the mixing bowl and cook in
the microwave for 5 minutes, stirring once during cooking.
Add the beetroot and cook for a further 2 minutes.
Meanwhile, to make a sauce, liquidise the breadcrumbs with
the soured cream until smooth and thick. Transfer to the
pudding basin and add the butter, nutmeg and seasoning.
Stir in the milk and cook in the microwave for 4 minutes,
stirring once during cooking.

Mix the cheese into the beetroot mixture and season
generously. Heat in the microwave for 1 minute, then place
both halves of the loaf shell on a serving dish and fill with
the beetroot mixture. Pour over a little of the sauce and
sprinkle with the chopped chives. Serve the remaining sauce
separately.

Lyonnaise potatoes

**Utensils: cook-bag, 1.5-litre/2½-pint shallow
ovenproof dish
Microwave cooking time: 15 minutes**

Serves: 4

METRIC/IMPERIAL

1 medium onion, thinly
  sliced
0.5 kg/1¼ lb potatoes,
  peeled and sliced 0.25
  cm/⅛ inch thick

salt and freshly ground black
  pepper
150 ml/¼ pint double cream
25 g/1 oz cheese, grated
Garnish:
few spring onions, sliced

Place the onion in the cook-bag and secure loosely with an
elastic band. Make a few snips in the bag to allow the steam
to escape. Cook in the microwave for 3 minutes.

Arrange alternate layers of onion and potato in the dish,
season and pour over the cream. Cover with cling film and
cook in the microwave for 5 minutes. Allow to stand for 1
minute and then continue to cook in the microwave for a
further 5 minutes. Remove the cover and sprinkle with grated
cheese. Return to the microwave and heat for a further 2
minutes or until the cheese has melted, or place under a hot
grill to brown the cheese if preferred.

Stuffed baked potatoes

**Utensils: kitchen paper, 1-litre/2-pint ovenproof
soufflé dish
Microwave cooking time: 18–20 minutes for
potatoes (time varies for different fillings)**

Serves: 4

METRIC/IMPERIAL

4 large potatoes, about 225 g/
  8 oz each
fillings:
a) Curried prawn
25g/1 oz butter
2 teaspoons curry powder
50 g/2 oz onion, chopped

2 tablespoons flour
150 ml/¼ pint milk
225 g/8 oz peeled prawns
salt and freshly ground black
  pepper

b) Celery and cream cheese
225 g/8 oz cream cheese
3 sticks celery, finely chopped
freshly ground black pepper

c) Apple and frankfurter
50 g/2 oz onion, grated
1 large eating apple, chopped
1 (170-g/6-oz) packet frankfurters, cut in chunks

¼ teaspoon sage
2 teaspoons cornflour
3 tablespoons water
2 tablespoons double cream
salt and freshly ground black pepper

d) Creamed avocado
2 ripe avocado pears
1 tablespoon lemon juice
2 tablespoons double cream
freshly ground black pepper
chopped chives

Prick the skins of the potatoes and place as far apart as possible on a double thickness of kitchen paper in the microwave oven. Cook for 18–20 minutes, depending on the size of the potatoes, rearranging 4 times during cooking.

Halve the potatoes and top with any of the following fillings:

a) Curried prawn In the soufflé dish melt the butter in the microwave for 1 minute. Add the curry powder and cook in the microwave for 5 minutes. Add the flour and mix to a smooth sauce with the milk. Stir in the prawns and continue to cook in the microwave for 5 minutes. Season.

b) Celery and cream cheese Mix together the cream cheese and celery, season with pepper and pile on to the halved potatoes immediately before serving.

c) Apple and frankfurter In the soufflé dish mix together the onion, apple, frankfurters and sage. Stir well and cook in the microwave for 2 minutes. Blend the cornflour with the water. add the cream and pour over the other ingredients. Heat in the microwave for a further 2 minutes, stirring twice during cooking. Taste and season before serving.

d) Creamed avocado Halve the pears, remove the stones and cream the flesh with the lemon juice and cream. Season with freshly ground black pepper and pile on top of the halved potatoes. Sprinkle with chopped chives before serving.

German potato salad

Utensils: cook-bag, 1.5-litre/2½-pint oval ovenproof dish
Microwave cooking time: 11 minutes

Serves: 4

METRIC/IMPERIAL

0.75 kg/1½ lb potatoes,
  peeled and cut into chunks
4 rashers streaky bacon,
  chopped
½ bunch spring onions,
  finely sliced
25 g/1 oz butter
1 tablespoon flour

salt and freshly ground black
  pepper
100 g/4 oz garlic sausage,
  cubed
150 ml/¼ pint single cream
Garnish:
poppy seeds
chopped chives

Place the chunks of potato in the cook-bag and secure
loosely with an elastic band. Make several snips in the bag,
to allow the steam to escape. Cook in the microwave for 5
minutes and leave in the bag to keep hot.

Place the bacon, onions and butter in the oval dish and
cook in the microwave for 5 minutes. Stir in the flour,
seasoning, garlic sausage and cream and heat in the
microwave for 1 minute. Stir in the cooked potatoes and
sprinkle with poppy seeds and chopped chives.

Cream-baked cucumber

Utensil: 1.5-litre/2½-pint oval ovenproof dish
Microwave cooking time: 10 minutes

Serves: 4

METRIC/IMPERIAL

1 cucumber, peeled
½ teaspoon dill weed
150 ml/¼ pint double cream

salt and freshly ground black
  pepper
4 tablespoons chopped
  chives

Quarter the cucumber lengthways then cut into pieces
approximately 5–7.5 cm/2–3 inches long. Place the pieces of
cucumber in the oval dish. Sprinkle on the dill weed and
pour the cream over the cucumber. Season lightly and cook
in the microwave for 10 minutes. Sprinkle with chopped
chives and serve hot.

Courgettes à la grecque

Utensil: 1.5-litre/2½-pint oval ovenproof dish
Microwave cooking time: 7 minutes

Serves: 4

METRIC/IMPERIAL

2 tablespoons oil
25 g/1 oz butter
0.5 kg/1 lb courgettes, sliced
2 cloves garlic, crushed
4 tomatoes, skinned and
  sliced

100 g/4 oz button
  mushrooms
Garnish:
chopped parsley

Place the oil and butter in the oval dish and melt in the microwave for 1 minute. Add the courgettes and garlic and mix well. Cover with cling film and cook in the microwave for 2 minutes. Stir in the tomatoes and mushrooms, cover and cook in the microwave for a further 2 minutes. Stir the vegetables thoroughly, bringing the outside vegetables to the centre of the dish and vice versa. Cover and continue to cook in the microwave for a further 2 minutes. Allow to cool slightly before serving.
Garnish with chopped parsley.

Courgettes with chicken sauce

Utensils: cook-bag, 1-litre/2-pint ovenproof
pudding basin
Microwave cooking time: 10 minutes

Serves: 4

METRIC/IMPERIAL

8 medium courgettes
2 tablespoons flour
1 chicken stock cube
300 ml/½ pint milk
25 g/1 oz butter
225 g/8 oz cooked chicken,
  chopped

Garnish:
2 tablespoons chopped
  chives
2 tablespoons grated
  Parmesan cheese

Place 4 courgettes in the cook-bag, secure loosely with an elastic band and cook in the microwave for 3 minutes. Repeat with the remaining courgettes.
Mix the flour with the stock cube and a little of the milk

until smooth. Gradually add the remaining milk and butter
and cook in the microwave for 4 minutes, stirring once
during cooking. Whisk thoroughly until smooth. Add the
chicken and taste for seasoning. There should be no need for
additional salt or pepper.

Slit each courgette lengthways, leaving some skin intact,
and open out to a 'v' shape on a serving dish. Place a little
sauce on each and sprinkle with chopped chives and grated
cheese.

Spinach au gratin

**Utensils: cook-bag, 1-litre/1½-pint oblong
ovenproof dish
Microwave cooking time: 11 minutes**

Serves: 4

METRIC/IMPERIAL

0.5 kg/1 lb spinach, washed, dried and shredded	3 tomatoes, skinned and sliced
1 small onion, grated	150 ml/¼ pint double cream
25 g/1 oz butter	Garnish:
salt and freshly ground black pepper	grated Parmesan cheese
pinch freshly ground nutmeg	chopped parsley

Place the spinach in the cook-bag and secure loosely with an
elastic band. Make several snips in the bag to allow the
steam to escape. Cook in the microwave for 4 minutes. Place
the onion and half the butter in the oval dish and cook in the
microwave for 4 minutes. Add the spinach, small pieces of
the remaining butter and seasoning. Top with the sliced
tomatoes and pour over the cream. Heat in the microwave for
3 minutes. Allow to stand for a few minutes before serving.
Garnish with Parmesan cheese and chopped parsley.

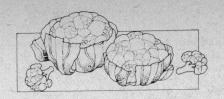

Cauliflower provençal

Utensil: 1.5-litre/2½-pint round ovenproof dish
Microwave cooking time: 20 minutes

Serves: 4

METRIC/IMPERIAL

1 cauliflower
1 tablespoon oil
1 clove garlic, crushed
1 small onion, finely
  chopped
1 (397-g/14-oz) can tomatoes
salt and freshly ground black
  pepper
few drops Worcestershire
  sauce
1 teaspoon chopped fresh
  marjoram
75 g/3 oz Cheddar cheese,
  grated
Garnish:
chopped parsley

Divide the cauliflower into small sprigs and place in the
ovenproof dish. Pour over 600 ml/1 pint boiling water and
cook in the microwave for 5 minutes. Drain well.

Using the same dish, add the oil, garlic and onion and
cook in the microwave for 3 minutes. Stir in the tomatoes,
seasoning. Worcestershire sauce, herbs and drained
cauliflower. Cover and continue to cook for 10 minutes,
stirring once during cooking. Sprinkle the cheese over the
top and return to the microwave for 2 minutes until the
cheese has melted. If liked, it can be browned under a
conventional grill just before serving. Garnish with chopped
parsley.

Broad beans with bacon

Utensils: cook-bag, 1-litre/2-pint ovenproof pudding basin
Microwave cooking time: 9 minutes

Serves: 4

METRIC/IMPERIAL

1 kg/2 lb broad beans,
  shelled
25 g/1 oz butter
1 small clove garlic, crushed

225 g/8 oz lean bacon,
  derinded and finely
  chopped
salt and freshly ground black
  pepper

Place the beans in the cook-bag, add 2 tablespoons of hot water and secure loosely with an elastic band. Cook in the microwave for 5 minutes, shaking the bag once during cooking. Leave the beans to stand in the bag for 2 minutes before opening.

Place the butter, garlic and bacon in the pudding basin and cook for 2 minutes. Season to taste and add the drained beans. Cook for a further 2 minutes before serving.

Vegetable curry

Utensils: cook-bag, 2.25-litre/4-pint ovenproof mixing bowl
Microwave cooking time: 14 minutes

Serves: 4

METRIC/IMPERIAL

350 g/12 oz cauliflower
  florets
225 g/8 oz carrots, peeled
  and diced
1 small onion, finely
  chopped
2 tablespoons grated root
  ginger
2 teaspoons ground
  coriander

1 teaspoon ground cumin
1 teaspoon turmeric
2 cloves garlic, crushed
50 g/2 oz butter
2 tablespoons flour
300 ml/½ pint pineapple
  juice
50 g/2 oz raisins
1 medium aubergine, diced
150 ml/¼ pint yogurt

Place the cauliflower in the cook-bag with the carrots. Add 2 tablespoons boiling water and secure loosely with an elastic band. Cook in the microwave for 6 minutes.

Place the onion, ginger, coriander, cumin, turmeric, garlic and butter in the mixing bowl and cook in the microwave for 2 minutes. Stir in the flour and pineapple juice and cook for 4 minutes, stirring once during cooking. Add the raisins and aubergine and cook for a further 2 minutes. Stir in the yogurt and serve with poppadums, plain boiled rice and grated fresh coconut.

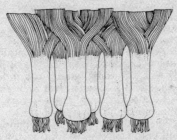

Leeks in creamy wine sauce

**Utensils: cook-bag, ovenproof serving dish, 300-ml/
½-pint glass measuring jug
Microwave cooking time: 9 minutes**

Serves: 4

METRIC/IMPERIAL

0.75 kg/1½ lb leeks, washed
   and trimmed
150 ml/¼ pint dry white
   wine
150 ml/¼ pint boiling
   chicken stock

3 teaspoons cornflour
3 tablespoons double cream
salt and freshly ground black
   pepper

Slice the leeks and place in the cook-bag with the wine. Seal loosely with an elastic band and cook in the microwave for 6 minutes.

Strain the leeks, reserving the cooking liquid, and place in the serving dish. Pour the cooking liquid into the measuring jug together with the stock. Blend the cornflour with the cream and stir into the stock. Season and thicken in the microwave for 3 minutes, stirring twice during cooking. Pour over the leeks before serving.

Asparagus in lemon butter

Utensils: cook-bag, 1-litre/2-pint pudding basin
Microwave cooking time: 10-12 minutes

Serves: 4

METRIC/IMPERIAL

450 g/1 lb asparagus
2 tablespoons hot water
100 g/4 oz butter
juice of ½ lemon

salt and freshly ground black
    pepper
grated Parmesan cheese
    (optional)

Trim off all the white woody part of the asparagus to give
even-length spears weighing approximately 350 g/12 oz

Lay the spears flat in the cook-bag, making sure that the
trimmed ends do not overlap. Spoon the water into the bag
and seal loosely with an elastic band. Cook in the microwave
for 5–7 minutes. Carefully open the bag and test the
asparagus with a knife. Cooking time may vary a little with
the thickness and age of the asparagus.

Place the butter and lemon juice in the pudding basin and
season well. Melt in the microwave for 5 minutes and pour
over the asparagus before serving. Sprinkle with a little
Parmesan cheese if liked.

Note: If the asparagus is left in the cook-bag with the elastic
band on, it will keep hot for up to 10 minutes.

Creamed artichokes

Utensil: cook-bag
Microwave cooking time: 12 minutes

Serves: 4

METRIC/IMPERIAL

1 kg/2 lb Jerusalem
    artichokes, peeled
1 tablespoon lemon juice
25 g/1 oz butter

salt and freshly ground black
    pepper
100 g/4 oz cream cheese

Place the artichokes in the cook-bag, add the lemon juice
and butter and secure loosely with an elastic band. Cook in
the microwave for 12 minutes and leave to stand in the bag
for 5 minutes.

Mash the artichokes with seasoning to taste until smooth,
then stir in the cream cheese. Serve immediately, either
sprinkled with a little freshly ground nutmeg or mace and
accompanied by Melba toast as a starter, or as a side dish
for the main course.

Vegetable cooking chart

Vegetable	Quantity or weight	Cooking utensil	Quantity of water or butter used	Microwave cooking time
Artichokes, globe	1 medium	cook-bag	4 tablespoons water	8-10 minutes
Artichokes, Jerusalem	450 g/1 lb peeled	cook-bag	2 tablespoons lemon juice 25 g/1 oz butter	10-12 minutes
Asparagus	450 g/1 lb medium spears trimmed	cook-bag	2 tablespoons water	5-7 minutes
Beans, broad	450 g/1 lb (shelled weight)	cook-bag	2 tablespoons water	5-7 minutes
Beans, French	450 g/1 lb	cook-bag	3 tablespoons water	7-8 minutes
Beans, runner	450 g/1 lb sliced	cook-bag	3 tablespoons water	5-7 minutes
Beetroot	4 medium	cook-bag	4 tablespoons water	10 minutes

Vegetable	Quantity or weight	Cooking utensil	Quantity of water or butter used	Microwave cooking time
Broccoli	450 g/1 lb	cook-bag	3 tablespoons water	7–8 minutes
Cabbage	450 g/1 lb shredded	cook-bag	2 tablespoons water	10 minutes
Carrots	225 g/8 oz in 1-cm/½-inch slices	cook-bag	2 tablespoons water	5 minutes
Cauliflower	225 g/8 oz broken in florets	cook-bag	4 tablespoons water	5 minutes
Corn on the cob	2 cobs, with husks removed	cook-bag	3 tablespoons water	8–10 minutes
Courgettes	450 g/1 lb sliced	cook-bag	25 g/1 oz butter	3 minutes plus 10 minutes standing time
Leeks	450 g/1 lb sliced	cook-bag	25 g/1 oz butter	5–7 minutes
Mushrooms, button	225 g/8 oz whole	cook-bag	25 g/1 oz butter	1½ minutes
Onions, whole	175 g/6 oz each (2 at a time)	cook-bag	2 tablespoons water	10 minutes

Vegetable	Quantity or weight	Cooking utensil	Quantity of water or butter used	Microwave cooking time
Parsnips	450 g/1 lb sliced	cook-bag	2 tablespoons water	10 minutes
Peas	450 g/1 lb (shelled weight)	cook-bag	2 tablespoons water	8 minutes
Potatoes, baked	1 kg/2 lb (4 large even-sized)	on kitchen paper	—	18–20 minutes
Potatoes, boiled	450 g/1 lb (in 50-g/ 2-oz pieces)	cook-bag	3 tablespoons water	5–7 minutes
Potatoes, new	450 g/1 lb (even-sized)	cook-bag	4 tablespoons water	5 minutes
Spinach	450 g/1 lb	cook-bag	—	5–6 minutes
Spring greens	450 g/1 lb	cook-bag	—	8 minutes
Swede	450 g/1 lb (in 25-g/1-oz pieces)	cook-bag	2 tablespoons water	10 minutes

Sauces, sweet and savoury

Sauces cooked in the microwave are always foolproof. No more burnt saucepans to wash up!

It is, however, important to use the recommended size of measuring jug or basin, as stated in the recipe. The sauce could boil over if too small a basin is used.

Most of these sauces can be made in advance and then reheated in the microwave just before serving. It really is worthwhile taking the trouble to make a sauce as it can add that special finishing touch to a dish.

Cumberland sauce

Utensil: 1-litre/2-pint ovenproof pudding basin
Microwave cooking time: 5 minutes

Makes: 450 ml/¾ pint

METRIC/IMPERIAL

2 tablespoons soft brown
    sugar
pinch cayenne pepper
150 ml/¼ pint hot chicken
    stock, made with a stock
    cube
150 ml/¼ pint red wine
1 tablespoon cornflour

3 tablespoons redcurrant
    jelly
grated rind of ½ small
    orange
2 tablespoons orange juice
salt and freshly ground black
    pepper

Place the sugar, cayenne, chicken stock and wine in the pudding basin and cook in the microwave for 3 minutes. Blend the cornflour with a little cold water and stir into the sauce. Add the remaining ingredients and continue to cook in the microwave for 2 minutes. This sauce makes an excellent accompaniment to gammon or pork dishes.

Tomato sauce

Utensil: 1-litre/2-pint ovenproof pudding basin
Microwave cooking time: 7 minutes

Makes: 450 ml/¾ pint

METRIC/IMPERIAL

15 g/½ oz butter
1 small onion, finely
  chopped
25 g/1 oz flour
1 (396-g/14-oz) can tomatoes
pinch basil
few drops Worcestershire
  sauce

salt and freshly ground black
  pepper
150 ml/¼ pint red wine
1 chicken stock cube,
  crumbled
2 tablespoons tomato purée
1 tablespoon chopped
  parsley (optional)

Place the butter and chopped onion in the pudding basin
and cook in the microwave for 2 minutes, stirring once
during cooking. Stir in the flour, then add the remaining
ingredients. Return to the microwave for 5 minutes, stirring
twice. Allow to cool slightly before liquidising. Reheat in the
microwave if necessary.

Bread sauce

Utensil: 600-ml/1-pint glass measuring jug
Microwave cooking time: 5–6 minutes

Makes : 300 ml/½ pint

METRIC/IMPERIAL

1 small onion, studded with
  6 cloves
300 ml/½ pint milk

75 g/3 oz fresh breadcrumbs
25 g/1 oz butter

Place the onion and the milk in the measuring jug and cook
in the microwave for 4 minutes. Remove the onion and stir in
the breadcrumbs and butter. Stand for 30 minutes. Reheat in
the microwave for 1–2 minutes. Serve bread sauce with game
and poultry dishes, especially at Christmas time.

Hot barbecue sauce

Utensil: 1-litre/2-pint ovenproof pudding basin
Microwave cooking time: 9 minutes

Makes: 200 ml/7 fl oz

METRIC/IMPERIAL

1 small onion, grated
4 tablespoons tomato purée
150 ml/¼ pint water
1 tablespoon wine vinegar
1 tablespoon Worcestershire
  sauce

2 teaspoons brown sugar
salt and freshly ground black
  pepper
2 tablespoons redcurrant
  jelly

Place all the ingredients together in the pudding basin and cook in the microwave for 9 minutes, stirring 3 times during cooking.

This sauce is delicious served with pork or lamb dishes.

Curry sauce

Utensil: 1.5-litre/2½-pint ovenproof basin
Microwave cooking time: 14 minutes

Makes: 450 ml/¾ pint

METRIC/IMPERIAL

1 onion, finely chopped
1 clove garlic, crushed
25 g/1 oz butter
1 tablespoon oil
3 tablespoons curry powder
1 tablespoon flour
2 tablespoons tomato purée
pinch ground cloves
2 tablespoons chutney

pinch cayenne pepper
salt and freshly ground black
  pepper
1 teaspoon lemon juice
1 teaspoon black treacle
450 ml/¾ pint hot chicken
  stock
few drops Worcestershire
  sauce

Place the onion, garlic, butter and oil in the basin and cook in the microwave for 4 minutes, stirring twice during the cooking time. Stir in the remaining ingredients and continue to cook in the microwave for 10 minutes, stirring frequently. Serve with all meat, fish or egg dishes.

Sweet 'n' sour sauce

Utensil: 2.25-litre/4-pint ovenproof mixing bowl
Microwave cooking time: 12 minutes

Makes: 750 ml/1¼ pints

METRIC/IMPERIAL

2 tablespoons oil
100 g/4 oz onion, coarsely
  chopped
100 g/4 oz green pepper,
  coarsely chopped
100 g/4 oz carrots, cut into
  strips
6 tablespoons tomato
  ketchup
2 tablespoons soy sauce
3 tablespoons dry sherry
2 tablespoons wine vinegar
1 (226-g/8-oz can pineapple
  chunks
1 tablespoon brown sugar

Heat the oil in the mixing bowl in the microwave for 2
minutes then add the onion, pepper and carrot and continue
to cook in the microwave for a further 5 minutes. Stir in all
the remaining ingredients and cook in the microwave for a
further 5 minutes.

Serve this tangy sauce with cooked pork, lamb, poultry or
fish.

White sauce with variations

Utensil: 600-ml/1-pint glass measuring jug
Microwave cooking time: 5 minutes

Makes: 300 ml/½ pint

METRIC/IMPERIAL

25 g/1 oz butter
25 g/1 oz flour
300 ml/½ pint milk

salt and freshly ground black
pepper

Melt the butter in the measuring jug in the microwave for 1 minute. Stir in the flour until well mixed then pour in the milk and stir well. Cook in the microwave for 4 minutes, stirring after every minute to prevent lumps forming. Season to taste.

Variations

Cheese sauce Stir 50 g/2 oz grated cheese into the cooked sauce.

Anchovy sauce Add 1–2 tablespoons anchovy essence to the cooked sauce.

Parsley sauce Stir 2–3 tablespoons chopped parsley into the cooked sauce.

Mushroom sauce Stir 50 g/2 oz chopped cooked mushrooms into the cooked sauce.

Onion sauce

Utensil: 1-litre/2-pint ovenproof pudding basin
Microwave cooking time: 9 minutes

Makes: 300 ml/½ pint

METRIC/IMPERIAL

25 g/1 oz butter
1 large onion, thinly sliced
25 g/1 oz flour

300 ml/½ pint milk
salt and freshly ground black
pepper

Place the butter and onion slices in the basin and cook in the microwave for 6 minutes, stirring twice during cooking. Stir in the flour, then add the milk and mix well. Return to the microwave for 3 minutes, stirring once. Season to taste. Onion sauce is delicious with lamb dishes.

Béchamel sauce

Utensil: 600-ml/1-pint glass measuring jug
Microwave cooking time: 8–9 minutes

Makes: 300 ml/½ pint

METRIC/IMPERIAL

1 small onion, quartered
1 carrot, thickly sliced
1 bay leaf
mace
10 peppercorns
few sprigs parsley

300 ml/½ pint milk
25 g/1 oz butter
25 g/1 oz flour
salt and freshly ground black
   pepper

Place the vegetables, bay leaf, mace, peppercorns, parsley and milk in the measuring jug and cook in the microwave for 4 minutes, or until the milk comes to the boil. Infuse for 30 minutes then strain.

Place the butter in the measuring jug and melt in the microwave for 1 minute. Stir in the flour, mixing well, and then stir in the strained milk. Return to the microwave for 3–4 minutes, until thickened, stirring every minute. Season to taste.

Apple sauce

Utensil: 1-litre/2-pint ovenproof pudding basin
Microwave cooking time: 2½ minutes

Makes: 300 ml/½ pint

METRIC/IMPERIAL

450 g/1 lb cooking apples,
   peeled, cored and sliced

2 tablespoons water
25 g/1 oz butter

Place all the ingredients in the pudding basin and cook in the microwave for 2½ minutes, stirring once during cooking. Sieve or mash the sauce until smooth. Serve with pork dishes and roast duck.

Brandy sauce

Utensil: 600-ml/1-pint glass measuring jug
Microwave cooking time: 2½ minutes

Makes: 300 ml/½ pint

METRIC/IMPERIAL

25 g/1 oz cornflour
300 ml/½ pint milk
25 g/1 oz castor sugar

15 g/½ oz butter
1 tablespoon brandy

Blend the cornflour with a little of the milk until smooth.
Place the remaining milk in the measuring jug and heat in
the microwave for 1 minute. Pour on to the blended cornflour
and then return to the jug. Cook in the microwave for 1½
minutes, whisking after 1 minute. Add the sugar, butter and
brandy, and whisk until smooth.

Chocolate sauce

Utensil: 1.75-litre/3-pint ovenproof pudding basin
Microwave cooking time: 2½ minutes

Makes: 300 ml/½ pint

METRIC/IMPERIAL

100 g/4 oz plain cooking
  chocolate
5 tablespoons golden syrup
3 tablespoons cocoa powder
3 tablespoons warm water
1 oz butter, melted

Place the chocolate, broken into pieces, with the syrup in the
pudding basin, and melt in the microwave for 2 minutes. In a
separate basin, blend the cocoa powder with the water and
butter. Add to the chocolate mixture and cook in the
microwave for a further 30 seconds.

Custard sauce

Utensil: 600-ml/1-pint glass measuring jug
Microwave cooking time: 7 minutes

Makes: 300 ml/½ pint

METRIC/IMPERIAL

300 ml/½ pint milk
2 eggs

1 tablespoon castor sugar
few drops vanilla essence

Heat the milk in the measuring jug in the microwave for 3 minutes, or until just boiling. Lightly whisk the eggs, sugar and essence. Pour the milk on to the whisked mixture, mix well and strain back into the jug. Return to the microwave for 4 minutes, standing the jug in a waterbath of hand hot water, stirring every minute. The custard should lightly coat the back of a spoon when cooked.

Egg and cheese dishes

Egg and cheese dishes cook particularly well in the microwave oven. Most of the recipes in this chapter take 10 minutes or less to cook, thus providing some good ideas for snacks.

There are two important points to remember when cooking eggs in the microwave. Firstly, you cannot boil eggs in their shells as they will burst, and secondly, foods that are egg and breadcrumbed become leathery.

Care must be taken not to overcook egg and cheese dishes as they can quickly become indigestible.

Kipper soufflé

Utensils: 1.5-litre/2½-pint shallow oblong oven-proof dish, 3.5-litre/6-pint ovenproof mixing bowl, 600-ml/1-pint glass measuring jug
Microwave cooking time: 10 minutes

Serves: 4–6

METRIC/IMPERIAL

225 g/8 oz frozen kipper fillets
1 small onion, chopped
grated rind of 1 lemon
1 tablespoon lemon juice
50 g/2 oz butter
50 g/2 oz flour
600 ml/1 pint milk

1 tablespoon chopped parsley
4 eggs, separated
salt and freshly ground black pepper
15g/½ oz gelatine
1 tablespoon hot water
Garnish:
chopped parsley
quartered lemon slices

Place the frozen kipper fillets in the oblong dish together with the onion, lemon rind and juice. Cook in the microwave for 3 minutes then turn the fish over and cook for a further 3 minutes.

Melt the butter in the mixing bowl in the microwave for 1 minute then stir in the flour. Heat the milk in the measuring jug in the microwave for 3 minutes then stir into the flour and butter. Whisk thoroughly and return to the microwave for 3 minutes, whisking every minute. Allow to cool slightly.

Remove the skin from the fish and liquidise the fish with the onion and any juices together with a little of the white sauce. Whisk the fish mixture, parsley and egg yolks into the sauce, taste and season.

Dissolve the gelatine in the hot water and whisk into the fish mixture then chill until half set. Meanwhile, prepare a 14-cm/5½-inch soufflé dish by tying a double band of greaseproof paper around the side of the dish to rise 5 cm/2 inches above the edge of the dish. Secure firmly.

Whisk the egg whites until they form stiff peaks then fold into the half set fish mixture and pour into the prepared soufflé dish. Allow to set then carefully remove the greaseproof paper. Press the chopped parsley around the sides of the soufflé and garnish the top with quartered lemon slices.

Scrambled eggs suprême

Utensil: 1.75-litre/3-pint ovenproof pudding basin
Microwave cooking time: 4 minutes

Serves: 4

METRIC/IMPERIAL

6 eggs
50 g/2 oz button mushrooms, chopped
25 g/1 oz cheese, grated

75 g/3 oz garlic sausage, chopped
3 tablespoons double cream
salt and freshly ground black pepper

Whisk the eggs in the pudding basin, add the mushrooms and cook in the microwave for 1 minute, stirring once.

Add the cheese, garlic sausage and cream, season lightly and return to the microwave for 3 minutes, stirring every minute, until almost set. Stir well and leave for 1 minute before serving with hot buttered toast.

Baked Vienna eggs

Utensil: 24-cm/9½-inch round ovenproof plate
Microwave cooking time: 4–4½ minutes

Serves: 4

METRIC/IMPERIAL

4 crisp Vienna rolls
4 short rashers bacon
4 standard eggs

salt and freshly ground black
  pepper

Cut the top off each roll and hollow out the soft bread from
the centre. Line each roll with a rasher of bacon and crack
an egg into the cavity. Season lightly and place 2 rolls on
the plate. Cook 2 rolls at a time in the microwave for 2
minutes to 2 minutes 15 seconds depending on how well
cooked the egg is liked.
Note: The bread scooped out from the rolls may be made into
breadcrumbs and dried or frozen for later use.

Stilton-baked eggs

Utensils: 4 150-ml/¼-pint ovenproof ramekin
dishes
Microwave cooking time: 3 minutes

Serves: 4

METRIC/IMPERIAL

1 (170-g/6-oz) packet frozen
  chopped spinach, thawed
100 g/4 oz Stilton cheese,
  crumbled

4 standard eggs
little grated nutmeg

Divide the spinach between the 4 ramekin dishes. Reserve a
little of the Stilton cheese and sprinkle the rest in the
ramekins on top of the spinach. Break an egg in each dish
and spinkle with a little nutmeg. Sprinkle the remaining
cheese over the eggs and cook two at a time in the
microwave for 1½ minutes, checking the eggs after 1 minute.
Serve hot with Melba toast.
Note: When cooking eggs in the microwave oven the timing
is particularly critical, as the eggs should be removed before
they are completely cooked.

Scotch eggs in herby cheese sauce

Utensils: 1-litre/2-pint shallow round ovenproof
dish, 600-ml/1-pint glass measuring jug
Microwave cooking time: 6 minutes

Serves: 4

METRIC/IMPERIAL

225 g/8 oz sausagemeat
75 g/3 oz onion, grated
4 hard-boiled eggs, shelled
50 g/2 oz fresh brown
  breadcrumbs
1 tablespoon flour
300 ml/½ pint milk

100 g/4 oz cheese, finely
  grated
1 teaspoon mixed herbs
salt and freshly ground black
  pepper
Garnish:
tomato wedges
watercress

Mix the sausagemeat with the grated onion and divide into 4
pieces. On a floured board, wrap each egg evenly in
sausagemeat. Roll the eggs in the breadcrumbs and place, as
far apart as possible, in the round dish. Cook in the
microwave for 3 minutes, turning the dish and eggs round 3–
4 times during cooking.

In the measuring jug, blend the flour with a little of the
milk and gradually whisk in the rest of the milk. Stir in the
cheese and herbs and heat in the microwave for 3 minutes,
whisking twice during cooking and at the end of the cooking
time. Season and taste the sauce before pouring over the
Scotch eggs. Garnish with wedges of tomatoes and sprigs of
watercress before serving.

Note: Eggs may NOT be boiled in the microwave oven as
steam builds up within the shell and causes the egg to
explode.

Coating with egg and breadcrumbs in the traditional
manner is unsuccessful in the microwave oven as the egg
coating hardens becoming rubbery and unpleasant.

Cheesy flowerpot loaves

Utensils: 6 7.5-cm/3-inch clay flowerpots
Microwave cooking time: 9 minutes

Makes: 6

METRIC/IMPERIAL

175 g/6 oz brown
  wholewheat flour
25 g/1 oz wheat bran
½ teaspoon salt
½ teaspoon dry mustard

50 g/2 oz Farmhouse English
  Cheddar cheese, finely
  grated
1½ teaspoons dried yeast
1 teaspoon sugar
300 ml/½ pint tepid water
1 egg, beaten

In a mixing bowl, mix together the brown flour, bran, salt ,
mustard and cheese. Dissolve the dried yeast with the sugar
in the water and leave in a warm place until it becomes
frothy. Whisk in the beaten egg.

Mix the yeast liquid into the dry ingredients and beat well
to form a soft mixture. Place a small round of greaseproof
paper in the base of each flowerpot to cover the hole. Divide
the mixture between the 6 flowerpots and cover with a piece
of polythene or cling film. Leave in a warm place until the
mixture has almost doubled in size.

Uncover the pots and cook in the microwave two at a
time, allowing 3 minutes for each pair. When cooked, slide a
knife between the bread and the flowerpot and turn out on a
wire rack to cool. Remove the greaseproof paper from the
base of the breads. Serve with butter and cheese or instead
of conventional rolls.

Note: These are best eaten on the day they are made.

Variations

Herby cheese flowerpot loaves Add 2 teaspoons dried mixed
herbs to the dry ingredients then proceed as for the basic
recipe.

Nutty cheese flowerpot loaves Add 50 g/2 oz chopped
walnuts to the dry ingredients then proceed as for the basic
recipe.

Cheesy fruit flowerpot loaves Add 50 g/2 oz sultanas to the
dry ingredients then proceed as for the basic recipe.

Mixed vegetables au gratin

Utensils: cook-bag, 2.25-litre/4-pint deep oblong ovenproof dish
Microwave cooking time: 19 minutes

Serves: 4–6

METRIC/IMPERIAL

350 g/12 oz cauliflower
  florets
2 tablespoons water
1 large onion, thinly sliced
1 large green pepper, cut in
  rings
25 g/1 oz butter
2 medium beetroot, cooked
  and chopped
salt and freshly ground black
  pepper

150 ml/¼ pint double cream
¼ teaspoon lemon juice
1 clove garlic, crushed
100 g/4 oz mature Cheddar
  cheese, grated
50 g/2 oz fresh brown
  breadcrumbs
2 hard-boiled eggs, chopped
1 tablespoon chopped
  parsley

Place the cauliflower and water in the cook-bag, secure the
end loosely with an elastic band and cook in the microwave
for 5 minutes. Remove the cauliflower to a strainer and place
the onion and green pepper in the bag with the butter.
Secure the end with the elastic band again allowing room for
the steam to escape, and cook in the microwave for 8
minutes. Shake the bag twice during cooking.

Place the beetroot in the bottom of the oblong dish and
arrange the onion and pepper on top, pouring over the butter
from the cook-bag. Place the cauliflower florets on top and
season well.

Mix the cream and lemon juice, add the garlic and pour
evenly over the vegetables. Mix together the cheese and
breadcrumbs and sprinkle over the top of the dish. Cook in
the microwave for 6 minutes, turning the dish 3 times during
cooking. Mix together the chopped hard-boiled eggs and
parsley and spoon down the middle of the dish. Serve hot or
cold.

Macaroni cheese de luxe

Utensils: 3.5-litre/6-pint ovenproof mixing bowl,
2.25-litre/4-pint ovenproof mixing bowl
Microwave cooking time: 31 minutes

Serves: 4

METRIC/IMPERIAL

225 g/8 oz macaroni, broken
  into short lengths
generous litre/2 pints hot
  water
1 teaspoon salt
50 g/2 oz butter
150 g/5 oz onion, finely
  chopped
25 g/1 oz flour

600 ml/1 pint milk
175 g/6 oz Cheddar cheese,
  grated
salt and freshly ground black
  pepper
paprika pepper
Garnish:
tomatoes, skinned and sliced
few sprigs parsley

Place the macaroni in the larger mixing bowl with the water
and salt. Cook in the microwave for 15 minutes, stirring
twice during cooking; drain and rinse.

Melt the butter in the smaller mixing bowl in the
microwave for 1 minute, then add the onion and continue to
cook in the microwave for 6 minutes. Stir in the flour to
absorb the butter then gradually mix in the milk. Add the
grated cheese and cook in the microwave for 5 minutes,
stirring twice during cooking.

Add the macaroni, season lightly and return to the
microwave for 4 minutes, stirring 4 times during cooking.

Transfer to a serving dish, sprinkle with paprika and
garnish with tomato slices and parsley before serving.

Potato pizza

Utensils: 1-litre/2-pint round shallow ovenproof
dish, 1-litre/2-pint ovenproof pudding basin
Microwave cooking time: 9 minutes

Serves: 4

METRIC/IMPERIAL

350 g/12 oz mashed potato
25 g/1 oz fine dried white
  breadcrumbs
1 teaspoon dried mixed
  herbs
salt and freshly ground black
  pepper
100 g/4 oz onion, chopped

50 g/4 oz green pepper,
  chopped
100 g/4 oz streaky bacon,
  chopped
1 (396-g/14-oz) can
  tomatoes, drained
175 g/6 oz cheese, grated
1 (50-g/1¾-oz) can anchovy
  fillets
few black olives

Mix together the mashed potato, breadcrumbs and herbs.
Season lightly and press in the base and slightly up the sides
of the round shallow dish.

Mix together the onion, green pepper and bacon in the
pudding basin and cook in the microwave for 5 minutes.
Arrange this mixture on the potato base. Top with the
drained tomatoes and grated cheese. Arrange the anchovy
fillets in a lattice pattern on top of the pizza and cook in the
microwave for 4 minutes, turning the dish 4 times during
cooking. Place an olive in each square of the lattice before
serving.

Cheese fondue

Serves: 4

METRIC/IMPERIAL

1 clove garlic
150 ml/¼ pint white wine
1 teaspoon lemon juice
450 g/1 lb Gruyère or
  Emmenthal cheese, grated

1 tablespoon cornflour
2 tablespoons brandy
pinch freshly ground nutmeg
freshly ground black pepper

Cut the clove of garlic in half and rub the cut sides around the inside of the fondue dish. Pour in the wine and lemon juice and heat in the microwave for 1–2 minutes until just hot. Stir in a third of the cheese, heat in the microwave for 1 minute then repeat with the remaining two-thirds of cheese, adding a third at a time and cook in the microwave for 1 minute in between. After the final amount of cheese has been added return to the microwave for 1 minute, stirring after 30 seconds. Blend the cornflour with the brandy and stir into the fondue. Season to taste and return to the microwave for 2 minutes, stirring frequently. Cool slightly before serving.

Serve with cubes of French bread, celery or florets of cauliflower to dip.

Note: A combination of Gruyère and Emmenthal cheese can be used if preferred.

If a fondue dish is not available, use a suitable casserole dish or a mixing bowl, but remember the cooking times may vary according to the dish used.

Egg custard

Utensils: 600-ml/1-pint glass measuring jug, 5 150-ml/¼-pint ovenproof ramekin dishes, 2.25-litre/4-pint oblong ovenproof dish
Microwave cooking time: 11 minutes

Serves: 4–5

METRIC/IMPERIAL

450 ml/¾ pint milk
3 eggs
75 g/3 oz sugar

few drops vanilla essence
freshly ground nutmeg

Heat the milk in the measuring jug in the microwave for 3 minutes. Add the eggs, sugar and vanilla essence and whisk lightly. Strain and pour into the ramekin dishes. Sprinkle each with a little nutmeg. Stand the dishes in the oblong dish filled with 600 ml/1 pint hand hot water. Cook in the microwave for 8 minutes, turning the large dish and the ramekin dishes 3–4 times during cooking. Leave to cool in the waterbath, then chill in the refrigerator.

Pizza crumpets

Utensil: 1.15-litre/2-pint shallow oblong flan dish
Microwave cooking time: 4 minutes

Serves: 4

METRIC/IMPERIAL

1 clove garlic, crushed	100 g/4 oz Cheddar cheese, cut into 4 slices
3 tablespoons tomato purée	
4 crumpets	1 (45-g/1¾-oz) can anchovy fillets
8 slices salami	
2 tomatoes, skinned and sliced	4 black olives, stoned and quartered

Mix the garlic with the tomato purée and spread over the crumpets. Divide the salami and tomato between the crumpets and top each one with a slice of cheese. Place the crumpets 2 at a time in the flan dish and cook in the microwave for 2 minutes each. Serve the crumpets garnished with anchovy fillets and black olives.

Rice and pasta

Rice and pasta may be cooked quickly and easily in the microwave oven, using the normal proportions of liquid. Fill the cooking utensil only half to three-quarters full for successful results. Small amounts of rice e.g. 100g/4 oz are successfully cooked in a 600 ml/1 pint measuring jug. The shape of the jug helps rapid cooking.

During cooking, rice and pasta need only occasional stirring and should be removed from the oven while they are still moist. Since a very high temperature is reached in the food, drying out will continue after removal from the oven, so they should be allowed to stand for a few minutes before serving.

Cooked rice freezes well and may be rapidly defrosted and reheated in the microwave oven. For best results the rice should be frozen in a cook-bag which may then be removed from the freezer, punctured (to allow any steam to escape) and then, discarding any metal clips, placed in the microwave oven to be reheated to serving temperature within minutes.

The type of rice used may alter the cooking time. Most successful are the long-grain varieties which cook by the absorption method. Brown rice may be quickly and successfully cooked in a microwave oven.

Lamb risotto with yogurt sauce

Utensil: 2.25 -litre/4-pint ovenproof mixing bowl
Microwave cooking time: 17 minutes

Serves: 4

METRIC/IMPERIAL

1 large onion, chopped
25 g/1 oz butter
450 g/1 lb minced lamb
225 g/8 oz long grain rice
2 tablespoons tomato purée
salt and freshly ground black pepper
1 green pepper, deseeded and chopped

600 ml/1 pint boiling chicken stock
Topping:
100 g/4 oz black olives, stoned and chopped
150 ml/¼ pint yogurt
2 teaspoons chives

Place the onion in the mixing bowl with the butter and cook in the microwave for 2 minutes. Add the minced lamb and rice and cook in the microwave for 5 minutes, stirring once during cooking. Stir in the tomato purée, seasoning, green pepper and add the stock. Cook in the microwave for a further 10 minutes, stirring 3 times during cooking. Mix the olives, yogurt and chives in a bowl and spoon over the lamb just before serving.

Rice and ham layer

Utensils: 600-ml/1-pint ovenproof pudding basin, 1-litre/2-pint ovenproof pudding basin, 1.75-litre/3-pint oval pie dish
Microwave cooking time: 12 minutes

Serves: 4

METRIC/IMPERIAL

1 large onion, chopped	½ teaspoon salt
25 g/1 oz butter	225 g/8 oz cooked ham
100 g/4 oz mushrooms, sliced	25 g/1 oz Cheddar cheese, finely grated
salt and freshly ground black pepper	1 egg
225 g/8 oz long grain rice	2 tablespoons milk
450 ml/¾ pint boiling water	1 tablespoon chopped parsley

Place the onion in the smaller pudding basin with the butter and cook in the microwave for 2 minutes. Add the mushrooms and season generously.

Place the rice in the 1-litre/2-pint pudding basin with the measured water and the salt and cook in the microwave for 8 minutes, stirring once during cooking. Layer the ham with the cooked rice and onion mixture in the pie dish, finishing with a layer of ham. Mix the cheese with the egg and milk and season lightly. Pour over the ham and cook in the microwave for 2 minutes, turning once during cooking. Sprinkle with chopped parsley and serve.

Spanish rice

Utensil: 1.75-litre/3-pint ovenproof pudding basin
Microwave cooking time: 22 minutes

Serves: 4

METRIC/IMPERIAL

100 g/4 oz onion, chopped
100 g/4 oz streaky bacon,
    chopped
2 cloves garlic, crushed
175 g/6 oz long grain rice
1 (190-g/6½-oz) can
    pimientos, drained and
    chopped

50 g/2 oz button mushrooms,
    sliced
1 chicken stock cube
450 ml/¾ pint boiling water
50 g/2 oz black olives,
    stoned
175 g/6 oz tomatoes, skinned
    and chopped

Place the onion, bacon and garlic in the pudding basin and
cook in the microwave for 5 minutes. Add the rice, pimientos
and mushrooms. Dissolve the stock cube in the boiling water
and pour over the rice mixture. Stir well and cook in the
microwave for 17 minutes or until the rice has absorbed
nearly all of the liquid.

Stir in the olives and tomatoes and leave to stand for 3
minutes before serving.

Savoury rice ring

Utensils: 2.25-litre/4-pint ovenproof mixing bowl,
1.75-litre/3-pint round casserole dish
Microwave cooking time: 36–37 minutes

Serves: 4

METRIC/IMPERIAL

50 g/2 oz butter
100 g/4 oz onion, chopped
100 g/4 oz green pepper,
    chopped
225 g/8 oz long grain rice
2 chicken stock cubes
600 ml/1 pint boiling water
Filling:
50 g/2 oz butter
100 g/4 oz red pepper,
    chopped

100 g/4 oz onion, chopped
225 g/8 oz raw chicken meat
salt and freshly ground black
    pepper
50 g/1 oz button mushrooms
juice of 1 orange
2 tablespoons dry sherry
2 teaspoons cornflour
2 tablespoons water
Garnish:
1 orange, segmented

Melt the butter in the mixing bowl in the microwave for 2 minutes then add the onion and green pepper and cook in the microwave for a further 4 minutes. Stir in the rice and the stock cubes dissolved in the boiling water. Stir all these ingredients together in the mixing bowl and cook in the microwave for 17 minutes or until the rice is practically dry. Press firmly into a greased 20-cm/8-inch ring mould and chill, overnight preferably.

Melt the butter for the filling in the round casserole in the microwave for 1 minute. Add the red pepper and the onion and cook in the microwave for a further 4 minutes. Roughly shred the raw chicken meat, season lightly and add with the mushrooms to the casserole. Continue to cook in the microwave for 2 minutes, stirring twice. Add the orange juice and sherry and cook for a further 2 minutes, stirring once. Blend the cornflour with the water and stir into the chicken mixture. Thicken in the microwave for 1 minute.

Turn the rice mould on to a serving dish and reheat in the microwave for 3–4 minutes or until fairly hot. Pile the chicken mixture into the centre of the ring and garnish with the orange segments.

Mussel paella

Utensil: 1.5-litre/2½-pint oval ovenproof dish
Microwave cooking time: 19 minutes

Serves: 4

METRIC/IMPERIAL

1 small onion, finely chopped	2 tablespoons chopped parsley
½ green pepper, finely chopped	1 tablespoon chopped chives
1 tablespoon oil	salt and freshly ground black pepper
225 g/8 oz long grain rice	2 (150-g/5¼-oz) cans mussels, drained
600 ml/1 pint hot chicken stock	3 tomatoes, skinned and chopped

Place the onion, pepper and oil in the oval dish and cook in the microwave for 5 minutes, stirring once during cooking.

Stir in the rice, chicken stock, parsley, chives and seasoning. Cook in the microwave for a further 10 minutes, stirring after 5 minutes. Add the mussels and tomatoes and heat in the microwave for a further 4 minutes. Remove to a heated serving dish, if liked.

Rice and vegetable salad

Utensils: 2 1.75-litre/3-pint ovenproof basins, 600-
ml/1-pint glass measuring jug
Microwave cooking time:
15 minutes: basic rice
10 minutes: spicy turmeric rice
22 minutes: brown rice

Serves: 4–6

METRIC/IMPERIAL

Basic rice:
225 g/8 oz long grain rice
600 ml/1 pint hot water
    (about 65°C/150°F)
1 teaspoon salt
Spicy turmeric rice:
100 g/4 oz long grain rice
300 ml/½ pint hot water
    (about 65°C/150°F)
¼ teaspoon turmeric
½ teaspoon salt
Brown rice:
100 g/4 oz brown rice
600 ml/1 pint hot water
    (about 65°C/150°F)

½ teaspoon salt
Vegetables:
sliced courgettes, red
    cabbage, shredded endive,
    tomato slices, watercress,
    shredded white cabbage,
    peas, grated carrot, cress,
    sliced aubergine and
    radishes.
Garnish:
sliced hard-boiled egg
soured cream
chopped parsley

Basic rice Place all the ingredients in the basin and cook in
the microwave for 15 minutes, stirring 3 times during
cooking. Allow to cool.
Spicy turmeric rice Place all the ingredients in the measuring
jug and cook in the microwave for 10 minutes, stirring
halfway through the cooking time.
Brown rice Place all the ingredients in the basin and cook in
the microwave for 22 minutes, stirring every 5 minutes
during cooking. Allow to cool.

Serve the cold rice on a large platter, alternating with a
selection of prepared vegetables. Garnish with slices of hard-
boiled egg and serve with soured cream sprinkled with
parsley.

Chicken rice salad

Utensil: 600-ml/1-pint glass measuring jug
Microwave cooking time: 10 minutes

Serves: 4

METRIC/IMPERIAL

100 g/4 oz long grain rice
300 ml/½ pint hot water
   (46°C/115°F)
1 chicken stock cube
225 g/8 oz cooked chicken
   meat, chopped

1 red pepper, chopped
75 g/3 oz cocktail onions
2 tablespoons capers
grated rind of 1 lemon
2 tablespoons mayonnaise
Garnish:
parsley sprig

Place the rice in the measuring jug together with the water
and crumbled stock cube. Cook in the microwave for 10
minutes and leave to stand for 5 minutes.

Stir the chopped chicken into the rice together with the
red pepper, cocktail onions, capers and lemon rind. Leave
until cold and mix in the mayonnaise. Turn into a serving
dish and garnish with parsley.

Rice cakes

Utensils: 1-litre/2-pint ovenproof pudding basin,
600-ml/1-pint glass measuring jug, 23-cm/9-inch
flan dish
Microwave cooking time: 14 minutes

Serves: 4

METRIC/IMPERIAL

100 g/4 oz easy-cook rice
300 ml/½ pint boiling water
¼ teaspoon salt
2 tablespoons flour
50 g/2 oz butter
150 ml/¼ pint milk
salt and freshly ground black
   pepper

225 g/8 oz cooked chicken,
   finely chopped
½ teaspoon nutmeg
Garnish:
Tomato wedges
parsley sprigs

Place the rice in the pudding basin with the boiling water and salt. Stir and cook in the microwave for 8 minutes, stirring once during cooking.

Place the flour and butter in the measuring jug and stir in the milk. Cook in the microwave for 3 minutes, whisking thoroughly once during cooking. Whisk until smooth, season to taste and stir in the chicken and nutmeg. Add the sauce to the rice and stir well to form a soft mixture. Cool and chill.

Divide the mixture into 8 portions and, with wet hands, form each portion into a small cake measuring approximately 6 cm/2½ inches in diameter. Arrange half of the cakes well apart in the flan dish and cook in the microwave for 1½ minutes, until hot. Carefully remove to a serving dish and garnish with the tomato wedges and sprigs of parsley for serving. Repeat with the remaining cakes.

Bacon and pasta casserole

**Utensils: 1-litre/1¾-pint glass measuring jug, 2.25-litre/4-pint ovenproof mixing bowl, 3.5-litre/6-pint ovenproof mixing bowl
Microwave cooking time: 26 minutes**

Serves: 4–6

METRIC/IMPERIAL

1 (500-g/1.1-lb) prepacked bacon joint, cubed
4 tablespoons cold water
100 g/4 oz pasta bows
½ teaspoon salt
900 ml/1½ pints boiling water
225 g/8 oz pickling onions
25 g/1 oz butter
1 chicken stock cube dissolved in 2 tablespoons boiling water

300 ml/½ pint red wine
salt and freshly ground black pepper
1 (397-g/14-oz) can tomatoes
1 tablespoon tomato purée
100 g/4 oz mushrooms, sliced
2 tablespoons chopped fresh parsley
2 tablespoons Parmesan cheese

Place the bacon in the jug, add the measured water, cover with cling film and cook in the microwave for 4 minutes. Place the pasta, salt and boiling water in the small mixing bowl. Cook in the microwave for 10 minutes stirring 3 times during cooking. Place the onions in the large mixing bowl with the butter and cook in the microwave for 4 minutes. Stir in the stock mixture and add the wine. Add the seasoning, canned tomatoes and tomato purée and cook in the microwave for 4 minutes. Stir in the drained pasta, bacon and the mushrooms. Cook for a further 4 minutes, stirring once during cooking. Stir in the chopped parsley and sprinkle with Parmesan cheese just before serving.

Stuffed cannelloni

Utensils: 1-litre/1½-pint oblong ovenproof dish,
1.5-litre/2½-pint oval ovenproof pie dish
Microwave cooking time: 19–20 minutes

Serves: 4

METRIC/IMPERIAL

1 small onion, finely chopped	225 g/8 oz mushrooms, finely chopped
1 tablespoon oil	8 tubes cannelloni
175 g/6 oz chicken livers, chopped	900 ml/1½ pints boiling water
1 (227-g/8-oz) can tomatoes	tomato sauce (see page 111) grated Parmesan cheese

Place the onion and oil in the oblong pie dish and cook in the microwave for 3–4 minutes, until the onion is soft. Stir in the chicken livers and continue to cook in the microwave for 3 minutes, stirring once. Add the tomatoes and mushrooms and cook in the microwave for a further 2 minutes.

Place the cannelloni tubes in the oval dish and pour over the boiling water, making sure the cannelloni is immersed. Cook in the microwave for 10 minutes, stopping half way through the cooking time to rearrange the cannelloni. Drain and stuff each tube with the filling, using a teaspoon. Return the cannelloni to the oval dish. Pour over the tomato sauce, making sure the cannelloni is covered. Sprinkle with Parmesan cheese and reheat in the microwave for 1 minute.

Creamed noodles with mushrooms

Utensils: 1-litre/2-pint round ovenproof dish, 1.5-litre/2½-pint round ovenproof dish
Microwave cooking time: 8 minutes

Serves: 4

METRIC/IMPERIAL

175 g/6 oz ribbon noodles
¼ teaspoon salt
450 ml/¾ pint boiling water
100 g/4 oz button
  mushrooms
15 g/½ oz butter

salt and freshly ground black
  pepper
150 ml/¼ pint double cream
Garnish:
poppy seeds
chopped parsley

Place the noodles, salt and boiling water in the smaller round dish, cover with cling film and cook in the microwave for 5 minutes, stirring after 3 minutes. Drain and rinse under hot water.

Place the mushrooms and butter in the larger dish and cook in the microwave for 1 minute. Stir in the noodles, seasoning and cream. Heat in the microwave for 2 minutes, stirring once. Garnish with poppy seeds and chopped parsley.

Curried macaroni with nuts

Utensil: 2.25-litre/4-pint ovenproof mixing bowl
Microwave cooking time: 22 minutes

Serves: 4

METRIC/IMPERIAL

175 g/6 oz cut macaroni
600 ml/1 pint boiling water
1 teaspoon salt
25 g/1 oz butter
1 large onion, chopped
1 tablespoon curry powder
1 tablespoon flour
2 tablespoons tomato purée
1 (396-g/14-oz) can tomatoes
100 g/4 oz mushrooms,
  sliced
50 g/2 oz sultanas
225 g/8 oz salted cashew
  nuts

Side dishes:
½ cucumber, peeled and
  chopped
1 small carton natural yogurt
freshly ground black pepper
1 red eating apple
2 bananas, sliced
juice of ½ lemon
2 hard-boiled eggs
2 tomatoes, skinned
few sticks celery
1 orange, segmented
chopped parsley

Place the macaroni in the mixing bowl, pour over the boiling water and add the salt. Cook in the microwave for 10 minutes. Allow to stand for 5 minutes before draining.

Using the same mixing bowl, melt the butter in the microwave for 1 minute. Add the onion and curry powder and cook in the microwave for 5 minutes. Stir in the flour then add the tomato purée, tomatoes, mushrooms, sultanas and cashew nuts. Continue to cook for 3 minutes in the microwave, stirring every minute. Stir in the drained macaroni and reheat in the microwave for 3 minutes, stirring 3 times.

To prepare the side dishes

Mix together the cucumber and yogurt and season with freshly ground black pepper. Place in a small dish.

Core and slice the eating apple, mix with the banana and toss in lemon juice to prevent discoloration. Place these in a separate dish.

Quarter the hard-boiled eggs and arrange in a dish with the quartered tomatoes.

Chop the celery and mix with the orange segments. Sprinkle with chopped parsley before serving.

Lasagne

Utensils: 2.25-litre/4-pint deep oblong casserole dish, 2.25-litre/4-pint ovenproof mixing bowl, 1.75-litre/3-pint ovenproof pudding basin
Microwave cooking time: 31 minutes

Serves: 4–6

METRIC/IMPERIAL

175 g/6 oz lasagne	Sauce:
generous litre/2 pints boiling water	50 g/2 oz butter
	4 tablespoons flour
1 teaspoon salt	600 ml/1 pint milk
25 g/1 oz butter	175 g/6 oz cheese, grated
1 large onion, chopped	½ teaspoon grated nutmeg
450 g/1 lb spinach, trimmed and chopped	450 g/1 lb tomatoes, skinned and sliced
salt and freshly ground black pepper	Garnish:
	tomato slices
	watercress sprigs

Place the lasagne in the oblong casserole and pour over the water. Add the salt and cook in the microwave for 10 minutes. Drain the lasagne and dry on kitchen paper.

In the mixing bowl, melt the butter in the microwave for 1 minute then add the onion and cook in the microwave for 3 minutes, stirring once during cooking. Add the spinach and season lightly then continue to cook in the microwave for a further 3 minutes, stirring every minute.

To make the sauce, melt the butter in the pudding basin in the microwave for 2 minutes then stir in the flour. Carefully stir in the milk and season lightly. Cook in the microwave for 7 minutes, stirring 4 times. Add the cheese and nutmeg, taste and adjust the seasoning if necessary.

To assemble the dish, in the deep oblong dish arrange layers of lasagne, spinach, sliced tomatoes and cheese sauce, ending with a layer of sauce on top. Heat the whole dish in the microwave for 5 minutes, turning the dish round 3 times, to reheat evenly. Brown under the grill if liked. Garnish with slices of tomato and sprigs of watercress before serving.

Creamed spaghetti with salami

Utensils: 2.25-litre/4-pint deep oblong casserole dish, 2.25-litre/4-pint ovenproof mixing bowl
Microwave cooking time: 24 minutes

Serves: 4

METRIC/IMPERIAL

225 g/8 oz short cut spaghetti	1 (198-g/7-oz) can sweetcorn
generous litre/2 pints boiling water	175 g/6 oz salami, sliced
	50 g/2 oz button mushrooms, sliced
1 teaspoon salt	100 g/4 oz frozen cut green beans
100 g/4 oz onion, thinly sliced	150 ml/¼ pint double cream
1 clove garlic, crushed	salt and freshly ground black pepper
1 tablespoon oil	

Place the spaghetti in the deep oblong dish, pour over the boiling water and add the salt. Cook in the microwave for 15 minutes and allow to stand in the water for a further 10 minutes before draining and rinsing with boiling water.

Mix the onion, garlic and oil together in the mixing bowl and cook in the microwave for 5 minutes. Add the sweetcorn, salami, mushrooms and green beans, and continue to cook in the microwave for a further 2 minutes, stirring once.

Stir in the cream and season lightly with a little salt and freshly ground black pepper. Heat in the microwave for a further 2 minutes, stirring once and then pour over the drained spaghetti. Toss well and place in a serving dish.

Spaghetti bolognese

Utensils: 2.25-litre/4-pint deep oblong casserole,
2.25-litre/4-pint ovenproof mixing bowl
Microwave cooking time: 35 minutes

Serves: 4

METRIC/IMPERIAL

225 g/8 oz short cut
  spaghetti
generous litre/2 pints boiling
  water
1 teaspoon salt
25 g/1 oz butter
225 g/8 oz onion, chopped
1 green pepper, chopped

100 g/4 oz mushrooms,
  sliced
450 g/1 lb minced beef
1 clove garlic, crushed
1 (397-g/14-oz) can tomatoes
2 tablespoons tomato purée
150 ml/¼ pint hot beef stock
grated Parmesan cheese
  (optional)

Place the spaghetti in the oblong dish and pour over the
boiling water. Add the salt and cook in the microwave for 15
minutes. Leave to stand in the water for 10 minutes before
draining and rinsing in boiling water.

Place the butter, together with the onion and green
pepper, in the mixing bowl and cook in the microwave for 5
minutes, stirring twice during cooking. Add the mushrooms,
minced beef and garlic. Mix together well before stirring in
the tomatoes, tomato purée and stock. Cook in the
microwave for a further 15 minutes, stirring every 2 minutes.
Serve the meat sauce on the spaghetti and sprinkle with a
little Parmesan cheese, if liked.

Pasta shells with seafood salad

**Utensils: 1.75-litre/3-pint round casserole dish,
1.75-litre/3-pint ovenproof pudding basin
Microwave cooking time: 17 minutes**

Serves: 4

METRIC/IMPERIAL

1 (190-g/6½-oz) can tuna in oil
1 onion, chopped
1 small green pepper, deseeded and chopped
100 g/4 oz button mushrooms, sliced
2 tablespoons tomato purée
juice of ½ lemon
few drops Worcestershire sauce
225 g/8 oz tomatoes, skinned and chopped
100 g/4 oz cooked mussels
salt and freshly ground black pepper
175 g/6 oz pasta shells
900 ml/1½ pints boiling water
1 teaspoon salt
4 tablespoons salad oil
2 tablespoons wine vinegar
1 teaspoon dried mustard
½ teaspoon salt
freshly ground black pepper
Garnish:
chopped parsley
lemon twists

Drain the oil from the can of tuna into the round casserole and add the onion and green pepper. Mix well and cook in the microwave for 7 minutes. Add the mushrooms, tomato purée, lemon juice, Worcestershire sauce, tomatoes and mussels. Season well and chill.

Place the pasta shells in the pudding basin and stir in the boiling water and salt. Cook in the microwave for 10 minutes and allow to stand for 5 minutes before draining and rinsing well with cold water. Drain thoroughly and chill.

In a screw-top jar or bottle, shake the remaining ingredients together until emulsified then pour the dressing over the pasta and toss well. Arrange the pasta in a ring on a serving dish and pile the seafood salad in the centre. Sprinkle with a little chopped parsley and garnish with lemon twists before serving.

Puddings and desserts

In this chapter the microwave oven shows just how versatile it can be. Whether you want ice cream, cheesecake or Christmas pudding for dessert, there is something here for every taste.

Christmas puddings are no longer the trial they used to be, as the microwave will cook a pudding in only 9 minutes!

Christmas pudding

Utensil: 1-litre/2-pint ovenproof pudding basin
Microwave cooking time: 9 minutes

Serves: 4–6

METRIC/IMPERIAL

75 g/3 oz butter
175 g/6 oz currants
100 g/4 oz raisins
100 g/4 oz sultanas
15 g/½ oz almonds, chopped
75 g/3 oz plain flour
pinch mixed spice
pinch nutmeg

75 g/3 oz soft dark brown
  sugar
2 eggs
rind and juice of 1 lemon
2 tablespoons black treacle
grated rind of 1 orange
1 tablespoon brandy
gravy browning to colour
  (optional)

Place all the ingredients in a mixing bowl and mix well together. Add a few drops of gravy browning if a dark pudding is preferred. Place in the lightly-greased pudding basin and cover with greased greaseproof paper, securing with an elastic band around the rim. Cook in the microwave for 5 minutes, then allow to stand for 5 minutes. Cook in the microwave for a further 3 minutes and stand for 5 minutes. Finally cook for 1 minute and allow to stand for a few minutes before turning out. Serve hot with brandy sauce (see page 116).

If keeping the pudding, loosely cover with cling film to prevent the surface hardening. When cold, wrap in the greaseproof paper and foil and place in an airtight container. *Note:* This pudding will keep for up to 2 months.

Remember, with a microwave Christmas pudding do not add the traditional coin to the mixture!

Date and walnut pudding

Utensil: 600-ml/1-pint ovenproof pudding basin
Microwave cooking time: 3½ minutes

Serves: 4

METRIC/IMPERIAL

50 g/2 oz butter or
  margarine
50 g/2 oz castor sugar
1 egg
50 g/2 oz self-raising flour

50 g/2 oz walnuts, chopped
50 g/2 oz cooking dates,
  chopped
custard sauce (see page 117)

Cream the butter with the sugar until soft and creamy. Stir in the egg and fold in the flour. Fold in the walnuts and dates and turn into the lightly greased pudding basin.

    Cook in the microwave for 3½ minutes, turning once during cooking. Allow to stand in the basin for 2-3 minutes before turning out onto a serving plate. Serve with custard sauce.

Scandinavian layer pudding

Utensils: 1.5-litre/2½-pint ovenproof soufflé dish,
2.25-litre/4-pint ovenproof mixing bowl
Microwave cooking time: 13 minutes

Serves: 4–6

METRIC/IMPERIAL

100 g/4 oz soft margarine
100 g/4 oz castor sugar
100 g/4 oz hazelnuts, finely
  chopped
100 g/4 oz flour
½ teaspoon almond essence
0.75 kg/1½ lb cooking
  apples

juice of ½ lemon
75 g/3 oz castor sugar
2 tablespoons water
300 ml/½ pint double cream
4 peaches, stoned and
  peeled

Beat the margarine and sugar until soft and fluffy then beat in the hazelnuts, flour and almond essence. Place the mixture in the soufflé dish and cook in the microwave for 6 minutes, stirring well every 2 minutes. Set aside to cool.

Peel, core and slice the apples and place in the mixing bowl with the lemon juice and sugar. Toss well, add the water and cook in the microwave for 7 minutes until the apples are soft. Stir twice during cooking.

Whip the cream until fairly stiff and reserve a little for decoration. Slice the peaches and reserve a few slices for decoration. Crumble the cooked nut mixture; if necessary this may be placed in a plastic bag and crushed with a rolling pin. Arrange layers of the crumble, apples, peaches and cream in a 1-litre/2-pint glass serving bowl ending with a layer of crumble. Decorate with the reserved whipped cream and peach slices. Serve warm.

Pineapple and ginger layer bombe

**Utensil: 1.75 litre/3-pint ovenproof pudding basin
Microwave cooking time: 4 minutes**

Serves: 4

METRIC/IMPERIAL

100 g/4 oz soft margarine	1 (226-g/8-oz) can pineapple
50 g/2 oz castor sugar	cubes
2 tablespoons black treacle	2 tablespoons dry sherry
2 standard eggs	300 ml/½ pint double cream
100 g/4 oz self-raising flour	Decoration
sifted with 1 teaspoon	crystallised ginger
ground ginger	

Beat together the margarine, sugar and black treacle. Carefully beat in the eggs, one at a time, and fold in the flour and ginger. Line the pudding basin with cling film, transfer the mixture to the pudding basin and cook in the microwave for 4 minutes, turning the dish once. Turn after 2 minutes and cool on a wire tray.

Mix together 2 tablespoons of the canned pineapple juice and the sherry. Split the cake horizontally into 3 layers and soak each piece in the sherry mixture. Whip the double cream until stiff and drain the pineapple cubes. Sandwich together the cake with double cream and pineapple cubes, reserving some cream for covering the cake.

Cover the whole of the outside of the cake with whipped cream and swirl into peaks with a fork.

Decorate with pieces of crystallised ginger.

Chocolate mallow fondue

Utensil: 1.75-litre/3-pint ovenproof pudding basin
Microwave cooking time: 3 minutes

Serves: 3–4

METRIC/IMPERIAL

100 g/4 oz plain chocolate   1 teaspoon lemon juice
175 g/6 oz marshmallows

Place all the ingredients in the pudding basin and melt in
the microwave for 3 minutes, stirring after each minute. The
chocolate may not have quite melted so allow to stand,
stirring occasionally. Serve with cubes of banana, small
macaroons and sponge fingers to dip into the fondue.
Note: This fondue is ideal for serving at children's parties,
but remember not to serve it too hot.

Compote of cherries

Utensil: 1.5-litre/2½-pint oval ovenproof pie dish
Microwave cooking time: 9 minutes

Serves: 4

METRIC/IMPERIAL

450 g/1 lb fresh cherries   grated rind and juice of 1
4 tablespoons red vermouth   orange
3 tablespoons redcurrant
  jelly

Place all the ingredients in the pie dish and cook in the
microwave for 9 minutes, stirring twice during cooking.
Allow to stand a few minutes before serving. Serve hot with
whipped cream.

Banana bake

Utensil: 1-litre/2-pint oval ovenproof dish
Microwave cooking time: 5 minutes

Serves: 4

METRIC/IMPERIAL

4 bananas, peeled
4 tablespoons undiluted
   orange juice, thawed

6 tablespoons white wine
1 tablespoon lemon juice
50 g/2 oz brown sugar

Slice the bananas in half lengthways then cut each slice in half. Place in the dish and add the remaining ingredients. Cook in the microwave for 5 minutes, stopping halfway to rearrange the fruit (so that the bananas in the centre are moved to the outside of the dish and vice versa). Serve hot with cream.

Caramelised oranges

Utensil: 1-litre/2-pint ovenproof pudding basin
Microwave cooking time: 12 minutes

Serves: 4

METRIC/IMPERIAL

4 large oranges
175 g/6 oz castor sugar
100 ml/4 fl oz cold water

150 ml/¼ pint double cream
1 tablespoon Grand Marnier

Peel the oranges and remove all the pith. Slice the oranges, remove any pith from the centre, and all the pips. Place the slices back together to re-form the orange shape, or, alternatively, arrange the slices in a serving dish.

Place the sugar and water in the pudding basin and cook in the microwave for approximately 12 minutes until it becomes a dark golden colour. The caramel may need stirring once or twice during cooking if uneven caramelisation occurs, but this should be avoided if possible. Pour over the oranges.

Chill the oranges overnight in the refrigerator and serve with the cream whipped with the Grand Marnier.

Crunchy apple crisp

Utensil: oval porcelain flan dish
Microwave cooking time: 5–7 minutes

Serves: 4

METRIC/IMPERIAL

3 cooking apples, peeled,
cored and sliced
4 tablespoons undiluted
orange juice, thawed
75 g/3 oz brown sugar

50 g/2 oz butter, softened
175 g/6 oz plain sweet
biscuits, crushed
Garnish:
orange slices

Place the apples evenly on the base of the flan dish and
spoon over the orange juice.

Lightly mix together the sugar, butter and crushed biscuits
and spoon over the apples. Cook in the microwave for 5–7
minutes, until the apples are soft. Garnish and serve hot with
cream.

Note: To thaw frozen orange juice in the microwave, place
the frozen juice in a 300-ml/½-pint glass measuring jug and
place in the microwave for 1 minute. Stir well.

Rhubarb and banana nut crumble

Utensil: 1-litre/1½-pint oblong ovenproof pie dish
Microwave cooking time: 9 minutes

Serves: 4

METRIC/IMPERIAL

275 g/10 oz rhubarb,
trimmed
50 g/2 oz castor sugar
2 bananas
little lemon juice

Topping:
50 g/2 oz butter
100 g/4 oz plain flour
50 g/2 oz brown sugar
50 g/2 oz toasted hazelnuts,
chopped

Slice the rhubarb to approximately 1–2-cm/½–¾-inch
lengths, place in the pie dish and sprinkle with the castor
sugar. Cook in the microwave for 5 minutes, stirring twice.
Slice the bananas and sprinkle with the lemon juice then mix
into the rhubarb mixture.

Rub the butter into the flour until it resembles fine
breadcrumbs, then stir in the brown sugar and toasted
hazelnuts. Sprinkle evenly over the top of the rhubarb
mixture and fork the top lightly.

Cook in the microwave for 4 minutes, turning the dish
round once, and leave for a few minutes before serving with
whipped cream.

Raspberry mousse

Utensils: 1-litre/2-pint ovenproof pudding basin,
3.5-litre/6-pint ovenproof mixing bowl
Microwave cooking time: 14–16 minutes

Serves: 4–6

METRIC/IMPERIAL

3 eggs, separated
75 g/3 oz castor sugar
300 ml/½ pint milk
150 ml/¼ pint double cream
15 g/½ oz gelatine
1 tablespoon hot water
300 ml/½ pint raspberry
  purée, sieved

Decoration:
150 ml/¼ pint double
  cream, whipped
chopped nuts
few whole raspberries

Lightly whisk the egg yolks with the sugar then stir in the
milk and cream. Pour into the pudding basin. Place the
pudding basin in the mixing bowl and pour about 1.5
litre/2½ pints boiling water into the bowl to reach the level
of the custard in the basin. Cook in the microwave for 14–16
minutes, stirring every 2 minutes for the first 12 minutes,
then every minute until the custard will coat the back of a
spoon. Cool slightly.

Dissolve the gelatine in the hot water and stir into the
raspberry purée. Carefully combine the custard and the
purée by very slowly adding the purée to the custard. Chill
until half set.

Prepare a 12-cm/5½-inch soufflé dish by tying a double
band of greaseproof paper round the edge to come 5 cm/2
inches above the top of the dish. Secure firmly with string.
Whisk the egg whites until they form stiff peaks then fold into
the half set mousse. Pour into the prepared soufflé dish and
chill until set. Carefully remove the greaseproof paper by
edging a knife between the paper and the soufflé.

Press the nuts on to the sides of the soufflé and pipe the
whipped cream round the edge. Decorate the cream at
intervals with whole raspberries.

Pineapple and orange turnabout

Utensil: 1-litre/2-pint oval ovenproof pie dish
Microwave cooking time: 10–12 minutes

Serves: 4–5

METRIC/IMPERIAL

1 (226-g/8-oz) can pineapple
slices, drained
glacé cherries
4 tablespoons undiluted
orange juice, thawed
110 g/4oz soft margarine
110 g/4 oz castor sugar

2 eggs
110 g/4 oz self-raising flour
Decoration:
150 ml/¼ pint double
cream, whipped
angelica

Line the dish with cling film and arrange the pineapple slices
decoratively on the base. Place a glacé cherry half in the
centre of each slice and pour over the orange juice. Place
the remaining ingredients in a mixing bowl and beat until
well mixed. Spoon over the pineapple, spreading evenly.
Cook in the microwave for 10-12 minutes, giving the dish a
half turn after the first 5 minutes. Turn out on to a plate and
decorate with rosettes of whipped cream and angelica.

Rice crème brûlée

Utensils: 1.75-litre/3-pint ovenproof pudding basin,
3.5-litre/6-pint ovenproof mixing bowl
Microwave cooking time: 21½–23½ minutes

Serves: 4–6

METRIC/IMPERIAL

225 g/8 oz long grain rice,
cooked omitting salt (see
page 132)
4 egg yolks
2 tablespoons castor sugar
300 ml/½ pint single cream

300 ml/½ pint double cream
175 g/6 oz castor sugar
100 ml/4 fl oz cold water
50 g/2 oz toasted whole
almonds

Place the cold, cooked rice in the pudding basin. Lightly
whisk together the egg yolks and the 2 tablespoons castor
sugar, stir in the creams and pour this mixture over the rice.
Stir well so that the rice is well mixed.

Place the pudding basin in the mixing bowl and pour 1
litre/2 pints boiling water into the outer dish. Cook in the

microwave for 10–12 minutes, stirring twice during the first 5 minutes and then every minute as the custard begins to thicken. Pour the rice custard into a shallow oblong dish and chill thoroughly.

Place the sugar and water into the cleaned pudding basin and cook in the microwave for 11½ minutes or until the sugar caramelises to a dark golden colour. Sprinkle the top of the chilled custard with the almonds and pour over the caramel to evenly cover the surface. Chill thoroughly.

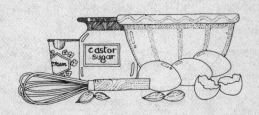

Crème brûlée

**Utensils: 1.5-litre/2½-pint ovenproof soufflé dish,
2.25-litre/4-pint deep oblong ovenproof dish
Microwave cooking time: 12 minutes**

Serves: 4

METRIC/IMPERIAL

4 egg yolks	300 ml/½ pint double cream
2 tablespoons castor sugar	75 g/3 oz soft light brown
300 ml/½ pint single cream	sugar

Lightly whisk together the egg yolks and sugar then stir in the single and double cream. Pour into the soufflé dish and then place the dish in the deep oblong dish.

Fill the larger dish with boiling water up to the level of the custard in the soufflé dish (about 1 litre/2 pints) and cook in the microwave for 12 minutes, turning the soufflé dish 3 times during cooking. Leave to cool.

Place the cooled custard in the refrigerator and chill thoroughly, preferably overnight. Carefully cover the top of the custard with the brown sugar and press down lightly. Place under a preheated grill until the sugar melts and serve immediately.

Spiced pears in mulled wine

Utensil: 1.75-litre/3-pint round ovenproof pie dish
Microwave cooking time: 10 minutes

Serves: 4

METRIC/IMPERIAL

4 ripe even-sized pears
600 ml/1 pint red wine (or
  use half water and wine)
pinch nutmeg
1 (5-cm/2-inch) stick
  cinnamon

50 g/2 oz sugar
pared rind of ½ lemon
few drops lemon juice
4 cloves

Peel the pears, leaving whole with the stalks on. Place the remaining ingredients in the pie dish and cook in the microwave for 5 minutes. Carefully place the pears in the hot wine and return to the microwave for a further 5 minutes. Leave to stand for 5 minutes before serving.

Grapefruit cheesecake

Utensils: 1-litre/2-pint ovenproof basin, 20-cm/8-inch china flan dish
Microwave cooking time: 4½ minutes

Serves: 4–6

METRIC/IMPERIAL

50 g/2 oz butter
125 g/4 oz digestive biscuits,
  crushed
175 g/6 oz cream cheese
2 eggs, lightly whisked
pinch salt
75 g/3 oz castor sugar
3 tablespoons undiluted
  grapefruit juice, thawed

vanilla essence to taste
almond essence to taste
100 ml/4 fl oz soured cream
Decoration:
150 ml/¼ pint double
  cream, whipped
grapefruit segments

Place the butter in the basin and melt in the microwave for 30 seconds. Stir in the crushed biscuit crumbs and mix well. Press into the flan dish, lining the base and sides evenly.

    Lightly whisk the remaining ingredients together until well blended and smooth. Pour into the flan dish and cook in the microwave for 2 minutes, turning the dish after 1 minute.

Cook in the microwave for a further minute, turning after 30 seconds. Allow to stand for 1 minute, then return to the microwave for 1 minute, turning after 30 seconds. Allow to cool, then chill in the refrigerator.

Decorate with whipped cream and grapefruit segments.

Variation

Use undiluted orange juice in place of the grapefruit juice.

Apple, apricot and almond sponge

Utensils: 1.75-litre/3-pint ovenproof pudding basin,
2.25-litre/4-pint ovenproof mixing bowl, 1-litre /2-
pint oblong ovenproof pie dish
Microwave cooking time: 43 minutes (see note)

Serves: 4–6

METRIC/IMPERIAL

225 g/8 oz dried apricots
600 ml/1 pint cold water
450 g/1 lb cooking apples,
  peeled, cored and sliced
25 g/1 oz castor sugar
50 g/2 oz soft margarine
50 g/2 oz castor sugar

1 egg
25 g/1 oz self-raising flour
½ teaspoon baking powder
25 g/1 oz ground almonds
50 g/2 oz toasted flaked
  almonds

Place the dried apricots with half the water in the pudding basin and cook in the microwave for 20 minutes, stirring 3 times. Add the remaining water and continue to cook in the microwave for a further 12 minutes, stirring twice.

Add the apples to the drained apricots in the mixing bowl and cook in the microwave for 5 minutes, stirring once. Transfer to the pie dish.

Place the margarine, sugar, egg, flour, baking powder and almonds in a mixing bowl and whisk thoroughly to give a light fluffy consistency. Spread this mixture over the fruit in the pie dish and sprinkle the toasted almonds over the top. Cook in the microwave for 6 minutes, turning the dish 3 times during cooking. Serve with whipped cream.

Note: For a quicker alternative, use drained canned apricots and omit the first 2 minutes cooking time.

Apricot truffles

Utensil: 1.15-litre/2-pint ovenproof pudding basin
Microwave cooking time: 3½ minutes

Makes: 14

METRIC/IMPERIAL

*100 g/4 oz butter or
    margarine, softened*
100 g/4 oz castor sugar
100 g/4 oz self raising flour
grated rind of 2 oranges
2 eggs
*6 tablespoons sieved apricot
    jam, warmed*

5 tablespoons orange liqueur
*1 (411-g/14½-oz) can apricot
    halves, drained*
50 g/2 oz cream cheese
1 teaspoon icing sugar
50 g/2 oz ground almonds
*50 g/2 oz blanched almonds,
    chopped and toasted*

Place the butter, sugar, flour, grated rind of 1 orange and
the eggs in the pudding basin. Beat well, using an electric
food mixer, until pale and creamy. Cook in the microwave for
3½ minutes, then allow to stand in the basin for 2 minutes.
When cold, crumble the cake and mix with the jam and 4
tablespoons of the liqueur.

Drain and dry the apricot halves on absorbent kitchen
paper. Mix the cream cheese with the remaining orange rind
and tablespoon of liqueur, the icing sugar and ground
almonds. Sandwich pairs of apricot halves together with this
mixture.

Press the cake around the paired apricot halves and form
into smooth balls. Roll in toasted almonds and chill lightly.
Serve as a dessert with whipped or clotted cream.

Crème caramel

**Utensils: 1-litre/2-pint ovenproof pudding basin, 4
150-ml/¼-pint ovenproof ramekin dishes, 2.25-
litre/4-pint deep oblong ovenproof dish**
Microwave cooking time: 16½ minutes

Serves: 4

METRIC/IMPERIAL

Caramel:
6 tablespoons castor sugar
*3 tablespoons hand hot
    water (about 48°C/120°F)*

Custard:
2 eggs
1½ tablespoons castor sugar
450 ml/¾ pint milk

Mix the sugar and water for the caramel together in the pudding basin and cook in the microwave for approximately 8 minutes or until the caramel turns a dark golden colour. It might be necessary to stir the caramel once during cooking if uneven browning occurs. Coat the base and insides of each ramekin with the caramel and set aside to cool.

Lightly whisk together the eggs and sugar for the custard and stir in the milk. Pour the custard into the ramekin dishes and place them in the oblong dish. Pour almost boiling water in the dish to surround the ramekins up to the level of the custard. Cook in the microwave for 8½ minutes, turning the large dish and ramekin dishes 3–4 times during cooking, until the custards are lightly set – they will become more firm on chilling.

Place the custards in a refrigerator to chill, preferably overnight. When required, turn out and serve with whipped cream.

Crunchy-topped coffee cream

**Utensils: 2.25-litre/4-pint ovenproof mixing bowl,
1-litre/1¾-pint glass measuring jug
Microwave cooking time: 5 minutes**

Serves: 4

METRIC/IMPERIAL

Topping	300 ml/½ pint strong fresh
25 g/1 oz butter	black coffee
50 g/2 oz plain flour	3 egg yolks
25 g/1 oz castor sugar	25 g/1 oz cornflour
50 g/2 oz chopped toasted	2 tablespoons milk
hazelnuts	2 tablespoons brandy
Coffee cream:	300 ml/½ pint double
50 g/2 oz demerara sugar	cream, whipped

Rub the butter into the flour in the mixing bowl. Add the sugar and hazelnuts and stir well. Cook in the microwave for 3 minutes, then leave until cold. For the coffee cream, dissolve the sugar in the coffee. Cream the egg yolks with the cornflour and milk in the measuring jug then gradually add the coffee. Cook in the microwave for 2 minutes, whisking once during cooking. Whisk thoroughly and allow to cool, covered with a piece of greaseproof paper or foil to prevent a skin from forming.

When cold, stir in the brandy and fold in the whipped cream. Turn into individual glasses and chill. Crumble the topping and sprinkle over before serving.

Vanilla ice cream

Serves : 4

METRIC/IMPERIAL

2 eggs, whisked
450 ml/¾ pint milk
175 g/6 oz castor sugar

1 tablespoon vanilla essence
300 ml/½ pint double cream

Combine the eggs, milk and sugar in the round dish and cook in the microwave for 6 minutes, stirring frequently. Allow to cool, then stir in the vanilla essence and cream. Pour into a freezing tray or a rigid shallow plastic container and freeze until semi-solid. Whisk again and return to the freezer. Allow to thaw at room temperature for 1–2 hours before serving.

Orange and apricot ice cream

Serves: 6–8

METRIC/IMPERIAL

1 (178-ml/6½-fl oz) can
 frozen orange juice
225 g/8 oz dried apricots
2 eggs

450 ml/¾ pint milk
175 g/6 oz sugar
300 ml/½ pint double cream

Place the orange juice in the measuring jug and melt in the microwave for 1–2 minutes. Add sufficient water to make up to 600 ml/1 pint. Pour into the mixing bowl with the apricots and leave to soak for 1 hour.

Whisk the eggs, milk and sugar together in the second mixing bowl and cook in the microwave for 5 minutes, stirring during cooking. Allow to cool.

Cook the orange juice and apricots in the microwave for 8 minutes, stirring once, and allow to cool. Stir the cream into the egg mixture, pour into a shallow rigid plastic container and partially freeze.

Liquidise the orange juice and apricots into a purée and stir into the partially frozen ice-cream. Freeze for 1 hour, whisk and then freeze until solid. Allow to thaw for 1–2 hours at room temperature before serving.

Preserves

Preserving is just another exciting aspect of microwave cookery, whether it be jams, chutneys or relishes.

No more messy, sticky saucepans or hot steamy kitchens to contend with; simply cook in an ovenproof mixing bowl, as stated in the recipe.

A jar of preserve is always a nice gift, and with a microwave oven it can be made quickly and easily without fuss.

To sterilise jars in the microwave oven. Half-fill each jar with water and heat in the microwave until boiling. Remove carefully as the jars will be hot, pour off the water and drain upside down for a few minutes before filling.

Testing for setting point of jam made in the microwave oven. There are two ways to test jams or jellies for setting point.

(a) Place a small spoonful of the jam on a saucer and allow to become cold. If it wrinkles when pushed with a finger, setting point has been reached.

(b) Stir with a wooden spoon and hold horizontally until a firm drip appears.

Whilst doing these tests, remove the jam or jelly from the microwave, as it may become overcooked.

Plum jam

**Utensil: 1.75-litre/3-pint ovenproof mixing bowl
Microwave cooking time: 21 minutes**

Makes: about 1 kg/2 lb

METRIC/IMPERIAL
*0.75 kg/1½ lb plums, stoned   450 g/1 lb castor sugar
and quartered*

Place the plums in the mixing bowl and cook in the
microwave for 5 minutes, stirring once. Stir in the sugar until
completely dissolved. Return to the microwave and cook for
16 minutes or until the jam has reached setting point. Stir
several times during cooking. Allow to cool slightly before
bottling in sterilised jars. Cover with circles of waxed paper,
seal and label.

Redcurrant and apple jam

**Utensil: 2.25-litre/4-pint ovenproof mixing bowl
Microwave cooking time: 28–33 minutes**

Makes: about 1.25 kg/2½ lb

METRIC/IMPERIAL
*450 g/1 lb redcurrants   350 g/12 oz cooking apples,
300 ml/½ pint water   peeled, cored and sliced
                                 1 kg/2 lb castor sugar*

Place the redcurrants and water in the mixing bowl and cook
in the microwave for 3 minutes. Stir in the apples and
continue to cook in the microwave for 5 minutes.
    Add the sugar and stir until dissolved. Return to the
microwave and cook for a further 20–25 minutes, stirring
occasionally during cooking, until the jam has reached
setting point. Bottle in sterilised jars, cover with circles of
waxed paper, seal and label.

Sweet orange marmalade

Utensil: 1.75-litre/3-pint ovenproof mixing bowl
Microwave cooking time: 25 minutes

Makes: about 0.75–1 kg/1½–2 lb

METRIC/IMPERIAL

2 large oranges	300 ml/½ pint boiling water
1 lemon	450 g/1 lb castor sugar

Coarsely grate the rind from the oranges and lemon. Cut the fruit into small pieces and place in the mixing bowl with the grated rinds and water. Cook in the microwave for 5 minutes. Add the sugar and stir until completely dissolved.

Return to the microwave and cook for 20 minutes or until setting point is reached. Stir twice during cooking.

Allow to cool slightly before bottling in sterilised jars. Cover with circles of waxed paper, seal and label.

Apple jelly

Utensil: 2.25-litre/4-pint ovenproof mixing bowl
Microwave cooking time: 33 minutes

Makes: about 1 kg/2 lb

METRIC/IMPERIAL

50 g/2 oz castor sugar	450 g/1 lb castor sugar
6 tablespoons commercial pectin	few drops lemon juice
750 ml/1¼ pints apple juice	few drops Angostura bitters

Place the sugar, pectin and apple juice in the mixing bowl and stir well. Cook in the microwave for 5 minutes, stirring once during cooking. Add the 450 g/1 lb sugar and stir until dissolved. Return to the microwave and cook for 28 minutes, stirring at 5-minute intervals, until a temperature of 96–98°C/205–210°F is reached, or when stirred with a wooden spoon and held horizontally a firm drop appears. Stir in a few drops of lemon juice and Angostura bitters. Bottle in sterilised jars. Cover with circles of waxed paper, seal and label. Keep in a cool place.

Apple butter

Utensil: 2.25-litre/4-pint ovenproof mixing bowl
Microwave cooking time: 15 minutes

Makes: about 1 kg/2 lb

METRIC/IMPERIAL

1 kg/2 lb cooking apples,
peeled, cored and sliced
25 g/1 oz butter
90 g/3⅓ oz sugar

pinch cinnamon
few cloves
150 ml/¼ pint water

Place all the ingredients in the mixing bowl and cook in the microwave for 15 minutes, stirring at 5-minute intervals. Remove the cloves, then mash the apple mixture until creamy. Bottle the apple butter in sterilised jars. Cover with circles of waxed paper, seal and label.
Note: Keep in the refrigerator for up to 3 weeks only.

Blackberry ketchup

Utensils: large cook-bag, 3-litre/5-pint ovenproof
mixing bowl
Microwave cooking time: 25 minutes

Makes: about 1 litre/1½ pints

METRIC/IMPERIAL

350 g/12 oz onions, chopped
1 kg/2 lb frozen blackberries
150 ml/¼ pint vinegar
½ teaspoon salt

1 tablespoon sugar
1 teaspoon mustard
pinch ground cloves
freshly ground black pepper

Place all the ingredients in the large cook-bag and secure loosely with an elastic band. Place the bag of ingredients in the mixing bowl and cook in the microwave for 25 minutes, rearranging the ingredients in the bag every 5 minutes.

Liquidise the mixture then cool it and press through a sieve. Place in clean, sterilised screw-top or clip-top bottles and store in the refrigerator for up to one month.

Tomato and apple relish

Utensils: 600-ml/1-pint glass measuring jug, cook-
bag 2.25-litre/4-pint ovenproof mixing bowl
Microwave cooking time: 38–43 minutes

Makes: about 0.75–1 kg/1½–2 lb

METRIC/IMPERIAL

200 ml/7 fl oz malt or wine
   vinegar
1 teaspoon pickling spice
1 kg/2 lb tomatoes, peeled
   and chopped
1 cooking apple, peeled,
   cored and sliced

1 small onion, finely
   chopped
salt and freshly ground black
   pepper
225 g/8 oz castor sugar
pinch ground ginger

Place the vinegar and pickling spice in the measuring jug
and heat in the microwave for 2 minutes, then strain.

Place the tomatoes, apple and onion in the cook-bag,
securing loosely with an elastic band. Cook in the microwave
for 6 minutes, stopping after 3 minutes to rearrange the
tomatoes, apple and onion, taking care to avoid the steam.

Carefully turn into the mixing bowl with the strained
vinegar, salt, pepper and sugar. Continue to cook in the
microwave for 30–35 minutes, until reduced. Stir in the
ginger to taste. Bottle in sterilised jars, cover with circles of
waxed paper, seal and label.

Cranberry relish

Utensil: 1.75-litre/3-pint ovenproof mixing bowl
Microwave cooking time: 10 minutes

Makes: about 350g/12 oz

METRIC/IMPERIAL

275 g/10 oz cranberries
1 tablespoon concentrated
   unsweetened orange juice

2 tablespoons wine vinegar
75 g/3 oz castor sugar

Place the cranberries, orange juice and vinegar in the
mixing bowl and cook in the microwave for 5 minutes,
stirring once during cooking.

Gently mash the fruit and stir in the sugar. Return to the
microwave and cook for 5 minutes.

Bottle in a sterilised jar, cover with a circle of waxed
paper, seal and label. Serve with poultry, game and
gammon.

Piccalilli

Utensils: 1-litre/2-pint ovenproof pudding basin,
cook-bag, 600-ml/1-pint glass measuring jug, 2.25-
litre/4-pint ovenproof mixing bowl
Microwave cooking time: 28 minutes

Makes: about 1.5 kg/3 lb

METRIC/IMPERIAL

225 g/8 oz cucumber, cubed
225 g/8 oz green tomatoes,
    chopped
225 g/8 oz onions, sliced
225 g/8 oz shallots, peeled
    and left whole
225 g/8 oz cauliflower florets
225 g/8 oz celery, chopped
generous litre/2 pints water
25 g/1 oz salt
25 g/1 oz flour

2 teaspoons dry mustard
¼ teaspoon turmeric
75 g/3 oz sugar
Spiced vinegar:
600 ml/1 pint malt vinegar
blade mace
few peppercorns
few cloves
pinch allspice
pinch cinnamon
pinch chilli powder

Place all the vegetables in a large bowl, cover with the
water and salt. Cover and leave overnight.

For the spiced vinegar, place the vinegar and all the
spices in the pudding basin and heat in the microwave for 8
minutes, stirring once. Allow to cool.

Drain and rinse the vegetables and place in the cook-bag.
Lightly secure the cook-bag with an elastic band and cook in
the microwave for 5 minutes.

Mix the flour, mustard, turmeric and sugar with a little of
the spiced vinegar to a smooth paste. Pour the remaining
spiced vinegar into the glass measuring jug and heat in the
microwave for 2 minutes, until hot. Pour on to the blended
flour, stir and return to the jug and cook in the microwave for
a further 2 minutes.

Place the cooked vegetables in the mixing bowl and pour
over the vinegar mixture. Cook in the microwave for 11
minutes, stirring twice during cooking. Allow to stand before
bottling in sterilised jars. Cover with a circle of waxed
paper, seal and label.

Green tomato chutney

Utensils: 600-ml/1-pint glass measuring jug, 2.25-litre/4-pint ovenproof mixing bowl
Microwave cooking time: 30 minutes

Makes: about 0.75 kg/1½ lb

METRIC/IMPERIAL

100 g/4 oz onion, finely chopped	½ teaspoon dry mustard
300 ml/½ pint vinegar	pinch ground ginger
450 g/1 lb green tomatoes, skinned and chopped	pinch salt
2 apples, peeled, cored and chopped	100 g/4 oz sultanas
	100 g/4 oz castor sugar

Place the chopped onion in the measuring jug with half the vinegar. Cover with cling film and cook in the microwave for 5 minutes. Transfer to the mixing bowl and add the tomatoes, apple, mustard, ginger, salt and sultanas. Cover and cook in the microwave for 10 minutes, stirring frequently.

Stir in the sugar and the remaining vinegar. Return to the microwave and cook for a further 15 minutes, stirring once during cooking.

Bottle in sterilised jars, seal and label.

Gooseberry chutney

Utensils: cook-bag, 1.75-litre/3-pint ovenproof mixing bowl
Microwave cooking time: 27 minutes

Makes: about 0.5 kg/1 lb

METRIC/IMPERIAL

450 g/1 lb gooseberries, topped and tailed	150 ml/¼ pint white vinegar
235 g/8 oz onions, finely chopped	1 teaspoon pickling spice, tied in a muslin bag
salt and freshly ground black pepper	175 g/6 oz castor sugar

Place the gooseberries and onions in the cook-bag, securing loosely with an elastic band. Cook in the microwave for 7 minutes, stopping after 3 minutes to rearrange the gooseberries.

Carefully turn out into the mixing bowl and stir in the remaining ingredients. Cook in the microwave for 20 minutes until reduced. Remove the bag of pickling spice and bottle in sterilised jars. Cover with circles of waxed paper, seal and label.

Rhubarb chutney

Utensil: 3-litre/5-pint oblong casserole dish
Microwave cooking time: 30 minutes

Makes: about 1 kg/2 lb

METRIC/IMPERIAL

450 g/1 lb rhubarb, sliced	150 g/5 oz soft brown sugar
50 g/2 oz raisins	pinch mustard
50 g/2 oz sultanas	pinch salt
few cloves	grated rind of 1 orange
4 onions	450 ml/¾ pint vinegar

Place all the ingredients in the casserole dish and cook in the microwave for 30 minutes, stirring every 5 minutes.

Bottle the chutney while still hot in sterilised jars. Cover the chutney with circles of waxed paper, seal and label.

Menus
and time plans

When cooking a complete meal in the microwave oven, timing needs to be very carefully planned, to allow the dishes to be separately cooked, yet still be piping hot and ready to eat when required.

Complete breakfast for 1
Total microwave cooking time = 4¼ minutes
Sausage, egg, tomato and bacon
(see page 166) — 2 minutes
Roll and butter
(see chart page 172) — 30 seconds
Coffee
(see chart page 173) — 2 minutes

ADVANCE PREPARATION
Place all the food on a plate and cover, either the previous night or just before cooking.
Note: If the food has been refrigerated overnight the microwave cooking time will need to be increased.

WHEN REQUIRED
Cook the food on the plate in the microwave.
Heat the roll and then the coffee in the microwave.

Luncheon for 4
Total microwave cooking time = 11–13 minutes
Scotch eggs in herby cheese sauce
(see page 121) — 6 minutes
Green salad
Crunchy apple crisp
(see page 146) — 5–7 minutes

ADVANCE PREPARATION
Hard-boil eggs and coat.
Prepare the remaining ingredients.
Prepare and assemble the salad.
Prepare and assemble the Crunchy apple crisp.

WHEN GUESTS ARRIVE
Cook the Scotch eggs in the microwave.
Make the sauce and finish the dish.
Serve.
Whilst eating the main course cook the dessert in the microwave.
Leave to stand for a few minutes before serving.

<h1 align="center">Luncheon for 4</h1>

Total microwave cooking time = 24 minutes

Mussel paella
(see page 131) — 19 minutes
Green salad
Banana bake
(see page 145) — 5 minutes

ADVANCE PREPARATION

Prepare and assemble the salad.
Prepare ingredients for the paella.
Make and assemble the Banana bake.

WHEN GUESTS ARRIVE

Cook paella in the microwave
Whilst eating the main course cook the Banana bake in the microwave and leave to stand before serving.

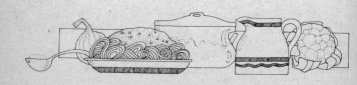

<h1 align="center">Dinner party for 4</h1>

Total microwave cooking time = 61 minutes

Grapefruit with vermouth
(see page 36) — 2 minutes
Rolled galantine of chicken
(see pages 82-3) — 20 minutes
Lyonnaise potatoes
(see page 98) — 15 minutes
Courgettes
(see chart page 108) — 3 minutes
Crème caramel
(see pages 152-3) — 16½ minutes
Coffee
(see chart page 173) — 4½ minutes

ADVANCE PREPARATION

Prepare and cook the Crème caramel the previous day and chill overnight.
Bone and stuff the chicken.
Prepare the grapefruit.
Prepare the vegetables for the Lyonnaise potatoes and cook the onions in the microwave. Arrange the onions and potatoes in layers in the dish.

Cook the stuffed chicken in the microwave and stand for 15 minutes.

Whilst the chicken is standing . . . pour the cream over the potatoes and cook in the microwave for 5 minutes, remove and allow to stand whilst cooking the grapefruit.

Return the potatoes to the microwave and continue with the cooking time.

Serve the grapefruit.

Remove the potatoes from the microwave and cook the courgettes whilst slicing the chicken.

Heat the coffee in the microwave.

Fondue party for 4
Total microwave cooking time = 10¼–11¼ minutes
Cheese fondue
(see pages 125-6) — 6–7 minutes
Garlic bread
(see chart page 171) — 1½ minutes (for 1 French loaf, cut in half)
Fruity mulled wine
(see page 167) — 3 minutes

ADVANCE PREPARATION
Make up the garlic bread. Grate cheese and prepare ingredients for the fondue. Prepare the ingredients for the mulled wine.

WHEN GUESTS ARRIVE
Heat the mulled wine in the microwave and allow to cool slightly before serving. Cook the fondue in the microwave. Allow to cool slightly whilst heating the garlic bread. Serve the fondue with a selection of dippers, such as carrot sticks, cauliflower florets, apple slices, etc.

Breakfast

**Utensils: 150-ml/¼-pint ovenproof ramekin dish,
23-cm/9-inch round ovenproof plate
Microwave cooking time: 2 minutes**

Serves: 1

METRIC/IMPERIAL

2 rashers streaky bacon	1 egg
2 chipolata sausages	1 tomato

Wrap the bacon rashers around the sausages and place on the plate. Butter the ramekin dish, break in the egg and stand on the plate. Add the halved tomato. Cook in the microwave for 2 minutes, turning the dish once.
Note: Cooking for 2 minutes produces an egg with a slightly soft yolk. If a very soft egg is required, the ramekin dish should be placed on the plate after 30 seconds cooking time.

Apple toddy

Serves: 6

METRIC/IMPERIAL

1 (929-ml/32.7-fl oz) jar concentrated apple juice	1 (5-cm/2-inch) stick cinnamon
1 orange, studded with cloves	freshly ground nutmeg
	3 tablespoons Calvados

Place the ingredients in the mixing bowl and heat in the microwave for 8 minutes, stirring once during cooking. Carefully remove the orange and discard the cloves. Slice the orange and float on top of the toddy. Serve hot.

Fruity mulled wine

Utensil: 1.75-litre/3-pint mixing bowl
Microwave cooking time: 3 minutes

Serves: 6

METRIC/IMPERIAL

1 bottle dry red wine	2 tablespoons clear honey
finely pared rind of 1 lemon	300 ml/½ pint port
finely pared rind of 1 orange	4 cloves
juice of 1 lemon	few slices orange and lemon
juice of 1 orange	

Pour the wine into the mixing bowl, add the lemon and orange rinds and juices. Stir in the honey and port, add the cloves and heat in the microwave oven for 3 minutes. Remove the fruit rinds and cloves, and add the orange and lemon slices just before serving.

Warming spicy wine

Utensil: 1.75-litre/3-pint mixing bowl
Microwave cooking time: 3½ minutes

Serves: 6

METRIC/IMPERIAL

1 bottle dry red wine	¼ teaspoon cinnamon
6 lumps sugar (or to taste)	150 ml/¼ pint brandy
6 cloves	little grated nutmeg
small piece root ginger	

Pour the wine into the mixing bowl and add the sugar, cloves, ginger and cinnamon. Heat in the microwave oven for 3½ minutes then remove the ginger and cloves. Stir in the brandy and sprinkle over grated nutmeg before serving.

Convenience foods cooking chart

Food	Quantity or weight	Cooking utensil	Amount of cooking liquid	Microwave cooking time	Special instructions
DRIED FOODS					
Apple flakes	35-g/1¼-oz packet 225 g/8 oz reconstituted	1-litre/2-pint ovenproof pudding basin	300 ml/½ pint cold water	3 minutes	Stir 3 times
Apricots	225 g/8 oz	1.75-litre/3-pint ovenproof pudding basin	600 ml/1 pint cold water	30 minutes	Stir 4 times
Beans, butter (soaked)	225 g/8 oz	2.25-litre/4-pint ovenproof mixing bowl	1 litre/2 pints boiling water	45 minutes	Stir 3 times
Beans, haricot (soaked)	225 g/8 oz	2.25-litre/4-pint ovenproof mixing bowl	1 litre/2 pints boiling water	40 minutes	Stir 4 times
Beans, green (quick dried)	(quick 32-g/1.1-oz packet	1.75-litre/3-pint ovenproof pudding basin	900 ml/1½ pints cold water	10 minutes	Stir twice
Beans, red (soaked)	225 g/8 oz	2.25-litre/4-pint ovenproof mixing bowl	1 litre/2 pints boiling water	45 minutes	Stir 4 times
Onions, sliced (quick-dried)	(quick- 40-g/1.4-oz packet	1-litre/2-pint ovenproof pudding basin	450 ml/¾ pint cold water	5 minutes	—
Peas, dried (soaked)	225 g/8 oz	2.25-litre/4-pint ovenproof mixing bowl	1 litre/2 pints boiling water	50 minutes	Add ½ teaspoon salt after 40 minutes

Food	Quantity	Container	Liquid	Time	Stir
Peas (quick-dried)	113-g/4-oz packet	1.75-litre/3-pint ovenproof pudding basin	900 ml/1½ pints cold water	13 minutes	Stir 3 times
Peas, split	225 g/8 oz	2.25-litre/4-pint ovenproof mixing bowl	1 litre/2 pints boiling water	40 minutes	Stir 4 times
Prunes (unsoaked)	225 g/8 oz	1-litre/2-pint ovenproof pudding basin	450 ml/¾ pint boiling water	20 minutes	Stir 4 times
SAUCES AND SOUPS (packet mixes, dried)					
Apple sauce	28 g/1 oz	1-litre/2-pint ovenproof pudding basin	200 ml/¼ pint cold water	3 minutes	Stir twice
Onion sauce	28 g/1 oz	600 ml/1-pint glass measuring jug	300 ml/½ pint milk	4 minutes	Stir 4 times
Asparagus soup	57 g/2 oz	1.75-litre/3-pint ovenproof pudding basin	600 ml/1 pint cold water	6 minutes	Whisk 3 times
Spring vegetable soup	28 g/1 oz	1.75-litre/3-pint ovenproof pudding basin	600 ml/1 pint cold water	10 minutes	Whisk 4 times
FROZEN FOODS Purchased					
Bread rolls	2	kitchen paper	—	1 minute*	—
Bread sliced	2 slices	kitchen paper	—	1 minute*	Turn over once
Chips, crinkle cut (cooked)	100 g/4 oz	1-litre/2-pint ovenproof pudding basin	—	2 minutes	Rearrange once

*Microwave defrosting time

Convenience foods cooking chart

Food	Quantity or weight	Cooking utensil	Amount of cooking liquid	Microwave cooking time	Special instructions
Cod, in butter sauce	170 g/6 oz	boil-in-bag	—	5 minutes	Pierce bag before cooking to allow steam to escape
Fish cakes	4 (225 g/8 oz)	large square rigid plastic microwave dish	—	4 minutes	Turn fish cakes over and round once
Orange juice, frozen	178-ml/6½-fl oz can	transferred to 300-ml/½-pint glass measuring jug	—	1 minute*	Stir once
Peas	450 g/1 lb	in the bag purchased in	—	8 minutes	Pierce bag to allow steam to escape
Pork chops	2 thick ones (2 cm/¾ inch thick)	polystyrene tray	—	3 minutes	Turn chops once. Resting time 15 minutes
Strawberries	225 g/8 oz	round flat ovenproof dish	—	2 minutes*	Rearrange fruit once

Home-made cooked dishes

Bread, garlic	½ French loaf (175 g/6 oz)	double thickness kitchen paper	—	1½ minutes	—
Casserole, beef	4 servings	round strong plastic dish	—	10 minutes	Break up the block of casserole as it thaws
Cottage pie	4 servings	oblong rigid plastic microwave dish	—	15 minutes	Remove dish from oven after 10 minutes. Cover with foil and rest for 5 minutes. Remove foil and cook for a further 5 minutes
Cheesecake	2 pieces (175 g/6 oz)	oblong strong plastic lid	—	30 seconds*	—
Complete meal: meat patties new potatoes peas gravy	2 (100 g/4 oz) 4 (150 g/5 oz) 100 g/4 oz 4 tablespoons	oblong rigid plastic microwave dish	—	8 minutes	Turn dish 4 times
Meat patties (raw)	4 (225 g/8 oz)	large square rigid plastic microwave dish	—	6 minutes	Turn patties over and round 3 times
Rice, long-grained, cooked	450 g/1 lb	In heavy weight polythene bag	—	8 minutes	Pierce bag to allow steam to escape

*Microwave defrosting time

171

Convenience foods cooking chart

Food	Quantity or weight	Cooking utensil	Amount of cooking liquid	Microwave cooking time	Special instructions
Sauces and soups					
Bolognese sauce	4 servings	place block in 1-litre/2-pint oblong ovenproof dish	—	12 minutes	Break up the block as it defrosts
Onion sauce	300 ml/½ pint	1-litre/2-pint ovenproof pudding basin	—	4 minutes	Break up the block as it defrosts
Apple sauce	150 ml/¼ pint	small solid plastic dish	—	3 minutes	—
Cauliflower soup	1 litre/2 pints	place block in cook-bag	—	18 minutes	Place the cook-bag in a large bowl to prevent spillage
REHEATING FOODS					
Bread, rolls	2	kitchen paper	—	30 seconds	—
Complete meal	(see frozen meal)	plain white round plate in cook-bag	—	3 minutes	—
Meat and potato pie (with pastry crust)	individual size	small round plate	—	1 minute	—
Steak and kidney pudding	individual size	upturned on small round plate	—	3 minutes	—

MISCELLANEOUS

Coffee, instant	1 teaspoon	300-ml/½-pint mug	250 ml/scant ½ pint cold water	2 minutes	Stir once
Gravy mix	3 heaped teaspoons	600-ml/1-pint glass measuring jug	300 ml/½ pint cold water	3 minutes	Whisk well twice
Jelly, orange	127-g/4½-oz tablet	600-ml/1-pint glass measuring jug	300 ml/½ pint cold water	3½ minutes	Stir twice Make up to 600 ml/1 pint with cold water
Porridge	100 g/4 oz	1.75-litre/3-pint ovenproof pudding basin	600 ml/1 pint cold water ¼ teaspoon salt 2 tablespoons sugar	5 minutes	Stir twice
Potato, instant	127-g/4½-oz packet	2.25-litre/4-pint ovenproof mixing bowl	600 ml/1 pint cold water 25 g/1 oz butter	4 minutes	Stir twice
Soya granules high protein e.g. Mince Savour	60-g/2¼-oz packet	1-litre/2-pint ovenproof pudding basin	150 ml/¼ pint cold water	1¼ minutes	Stir once
Spaghetti	40 g/1½ oz	600 ml/1-pint glass measuring jug	300 ml/½ pint cold water	3 minutes	Stir 3 times
Sponge cake mix	184-g/6½-oz packet	1.5-litre/2½-pint ovenproof soufflé dish	2 eggs	3 minutes	Turn dish 3 times. Resting time 3 minutes (after cooking)

*Microwave defrosting time

173

Index